The Story of Israel

Ronny Simon

Edited by - Kenneth Ortize

ISBN 978-965-91207-0-3

Ronny Simon
Israel Seminars
Seminars. Workshops, Lectures,
Computerized presentations.

Tel.: 972-2-5354443
Fax: 972-2-5900747
e-mail: r_guide@hotmail.com
web page: www.bepartofhistory.com

Printed in Jerusalem, 2008

The Story of ISRAEL

One land, many civilizations, one promise
4000 years of history

Ronny Simon

Jerusalem 2008

This book was written with the assistance of a friend, pastor and scholar, Ken Ortize.

His editing and the useful and clever advises made the publishing of this study possible.

Ronny Simon

Contents

Introduction

It would be pretentious, and in my opinion impossible, to cover 4000 years of history in a short study, especially when it is a history of the land of Israel.

One of the main goals of this study is to focus on the larger impact that other cultures had on the Jewish nation during the time the Jews were in possession of the land. Therefore, this study will not cover Israel's history in a detailed, chronological fashion. It will focus instead on the main eras, leaving out those that were too short to leave a significant mark.

It is a common mistake to consider the history of the land of Israel as synonymous with the history of the Jews – the nation of Israel. However, over the centuries, the land of Israel has hosted several major empires and numerous wars and religious clashes on its soil. Most of these episodes had little to do with the Jewish nation. Very few Jews lived in Israel during these events, and therefore did not figure significantly in them.

At the same time, knowledge of the geopolitical situation and an awareness of the location of the land are vital in obtaining an understanding of its past. Israel's geography and demographics are uniquely linked to its history.

For centuries, the more sophisticated cultures in the land dwelt on the plains, while the less developed cultures lived on the mountains. That was certainly the case when the Israelites and the Philistines clashed. The Israelites, a far less organized and equipped people, lived on the mountains; the more advanced Philistines lived on the plains.

This was also true centuries later when the Jewish and Greek cultures collided. The new, sprawling Greek cities were built on the lowlands and the plains; the Jews stayed in the mountain regions in an effort to maintain their isolation. Thus the geography of the land had a particular effect on the shaping of its history and the ongoing development of its culture.

Even today, one could argue that this foundation still underpins Israel. Most of the Jewish cities and farmland are on the plains, while the majority of Arabs live on the mountains.

The Bible Tells Me So

"...There, a people dwelling alone, not reckoning itself among the nations." (Numbers 23:9)

The Bible is one of our best sources of historical information about the ancient Middle East. Still, it does not mention several important events that shaped the land of Israel.

This is because, from the time of Abraham, the Bible's focus stays consistently on the nation of Israel, the Jewish people. The other peoples and the network of city-states that covered the land are mentioned only insofar as they affect the Jews.

For example, the region's commerce was bound up with world diplomacy under Egyptian influence, but the book of Genesis makes no mention of this fact. Yet Abraham lived under the effects of this and more while he traveled the length and breadth of Canaan – the future land of Israel.

During the 430 years the descendents of Abraham spent in Egypt, the Bible completely ignores the developing land of Canaan. But commerce and conflict continued to imprint its soil, and when the tribes of Israel finally returned four centuries later, it was to a very different place from the land their forefathers had known.

The Biblical books of 1st & 2nd Kings and some of the books of the Prophets cover Israel's history after this return, chronicling the nation's struggle for survival. At the same time, the Bible makes small mention of the very delicate political and diplomatic situations that the kings of Israel had to carefully navigate in order to survive.

For example, the Israelite King Ahab joined a coalition of armies to fight against Assyria (around 854 B.C.). This coalition succeeded in halting the Assyrian expansion for nearly a century, but the Bible doesn't speak of this. Because of the Bible's exclusionary focus on the Jewish people, we must look elsewhere for a detailed glimpse of the other cultures that scattered themselves across Israel's mountains and plains.

As we examine the broad effect of history on the land of Israel, it is my hope that the singular nature of this strip of small earth will imprint itself on your mind and expand your understanding of the land: the Israel of yesterday, today, and the future.

1

Setting the Scene
The Fertile Crescent

The land of Israel is a short ribbon of coastline situated along the eastern edge of the Mediterranean. It is about 60 miles wide, sandwiched between the sea on the west and the desert on the east.

This small, narrow piece of land has an amazing variety of flora and fauna, flourishing in four distinct climates. A day's travel will take you from the heavy snows atop Mount Hermon in the north, through the lush verdant hills and valleys of Galilee, down into the pastures and orchards of Samaria – and deposit you in the hot dry desert of the south: the lower Jordan valley.

Abundant rainfall on the high mountains provides a steady flow of water to provision the lowland springs. Melted snow courses down from the heights of Mount Hermon and feeds into the River Jordan, ending its journey in the Sea of Galilee.

However, the springs and rivers of Israel are few in number, and consequently guarantee a steady water supply for only a small number of people. Historically, these limited water sources, combined with mountainous cleft land and the lack of land suitable for large-scale farming, created an amazing patchwork of nations, city-states, small kingdoms and nomadic clans. Because of these naturally occurring geographic boundaries, no central authority was able to establish control over the entire land.

Israel is bridge as well as bottleneck. Dividing dry desert from deep sea, it provided the only accessible land route between its two powerful neighbors: Mesopotamia and Egypt. Each figured prominently in the history of the area.

Mesopotamia

Situated directly north of Israel, Mesopotamia means "the land between the two rivers." So named because it lies roughly encircled by the Tigris and Euphrates rivers, this area has come to be known as "The Fertile Crescent."

The two rivers are fed by the snow and rain that fall on the mountains of Armenia. Between sixty-five to seventy billion cubic meters of water sluice down from these mountains and flow into the rivers – bound for the dark, rich soil of Mesopotamia's southern plains.

The vast amount of water provided by the embrace of these two rivers allowed the land to produce bountifully despite its hot desert climate, and encouraged large numbers of people to settle along the shores of both waterways.

Every aspect of life was directly connected to the rivers. The hot weather guaranteed a year-round growing season and multiple harvests, and the Tigris and Euphrates both proved easily navigable. This became even more important as competing nations sought to control the area.

Since the land was able to sustain large populations, increased trade could also be sustained, which in turn allowed the local economy to continue its expansion. Because all of these conditions encouraged uninterrupted growth, settlements along major water sources typically developed into the largest empires of the ancient world.

Egypt

To the south of Israel lay Egypt: "the gift of the Nile." Ancient Egypt flourished along the banks of a mighty river, just as the civilizations of Mesopotamia did. As with Mesopotamia, the dense riverbank settlements made the task of controlling the population relatively easy.

Egypt differed from Mesopotamia in some ways: its people dwelt almost exclusively along the banks of the Nile (unlike the more broadly settled Mesopotamia), and it had no neighboring powers grappling for control. (In Mesopotamia, competing nations continually challenged each other throughout ancient times.)

Between a Rock and a Hard Place

With the powers of Mesopotamia and Egypt standing sentinel, it would be appropriate to describe Israel's situation through most of its history as "between a rock and a hard place." The land served as a buffer zone during the tenure of the earlier Canaanite city-states as well as the later Israelite kingdoms.

The inhabitants of the land were compelled to carve out their political existence very carefully. Allying with either power made them the enemy of the other. The Sidoneans, the Arameans, the Israelites, and the others who dwelt in the land lived constantly in the shadow of the mightier nations of Mesopotamia and Egypt.

Mesopotamia was more vulnerable than Egypt. From the east, from the heights of Asia, came continual throngs of nomads and nations, seeking food, water, and grazing land. These massive migrations shook the foundations of many Mesopotamian empires and eventually led to their downfalls.

Egypt, on the other hand, was surrounded by arid wasteland on all sides. To reach the coveted fertile land along the Nile River, it was necessary to first cross the vast, inhospitable desert. This made a successful invasion of Egypt almost impossible.

When either Egypt or the Mesopotamian powers were engaged in their own conflicts, their attentions turned inward and this allowed peoples in the land of Israel to rebel against their current overlords and gain their independence. The Israelites would occasionally be able to expand their territory and become, for a short time, a significant force in the region. But it never lasted more than few decades, for after the empires of Mesopotamia and Egypt recovered from their internal problems, they would once again assert their control in the region. The Bible often states that at such times, God was using these powers to punish Israel for their sins.

The desire to maintain or obtain full control of international byways has always been one of the main reasons for war. Whoever controls such byways controls world commerce, and thus is able to dominate other nations through sheer economic supremacy.

Unfortunately for the Israelites, the international road system crossed their land. All the trade, commerce, and communication between the empires to its north and south had to first pass through Israel. This was a blessing in times of peace (it strengthened the local economy), but Israel always lived with the knowledge that its strategic position was a constant source of temptation to stronger nations hungry for greater power.

Thus, Israel endured an endless number of armies crossing the land. These armies were usually marching through to confront another enemy, and so merited only a footnote in Israel's history. When their aim was war on Israel's soil, however, they left a more lasting mark: Israel's food stores were often exhausted and its forests were leveled. More limited resources were sometimes completely consumed.

At other times, when Israel was the objective of an invasion, large numbers of civilians followed these armies and would afterward settle in the land. These immigrants stirred new languages and other cultural changes into the melting pot.

This happened when the Israelites conquered the land in Joshua's time, and also during the Philistine invasion in the days of Saul and David. The Greeks infused their own culture when they conquered the land under Alexander the Great; the European Crusaders did the same. Even the founding of modern Israel changed the character of the land through the addition of foreign cultures.

In summary, the history of the land of Israel includes the nations and cultures that have lived there and the cities and roads they left behind. It includes the invading armies that pressed their cultural footprints into the soil. And above all, it includes the return of the Jews to their homeland and the establishment of the new State of Israel.

2

The Canaanite Era
c. 1800 – 1020 B.C.

The Canaanite era covers approximately 800 years. Although the area was under Egyptian control during this time, the Egyptian army was deployed far from Canaan, and the land, populated by a patchwork of independent city-states, was under no central authority or army.

Each city was responsible for its own fortifications. When these city-states were faced with immediate danger, they had to stand firm until the Egyptian army could come to their rescue. This forced each city-state to be well stocked with provisions, enough to withstand a long siege.

The Egyptian strategy was to ensure that Canaan remained divided, each ruler dependent upon Pharaoh. Therefore, Egypt encouraged rivalry between the various Canaanite city-states. This strategy was meant to prevent a coalition from forming to challenge Egypt. It was largely successful.

Still, there were times when the city-states did rebel. As a consequence, there were several Egyptian military expeditions to Canaan in order to suppress these revolts. Sometimes the Egyptian army would march to Canaan simply to showcase the might of Egypt, and so discourage a potential revolt.

But Egypt was not the only power the Canaanites had to contend with. Other strong kingdoms, although further away, were also interested in the land. Exploiting the Canaanites' desire for independence, these kingdoms would offer their help in an attempt to instigate the locals against one another and against Egypt. Their intent, of course, was to gain their own hold in the region.

Amuru Invasion

> *"And Terah took his son Abram, and his grandson Lot... and they went out with them from Ur of the Chaldeans to go to the land of Canaan." (Genesis 11:31)*

Archeological excavations throughout the land give evidence of a sudden destruction that occurred as a result of an invasion to the area. This was probably the work of the Amorites. Documents from Acadia speak about a nation called the Amuru, "the people of the west." These are the Biblical Amorites, descendants of Ham's son Canaan, who eventually destroyed the Acadian and Sumerian cultures in Mesopotamia.

The Amorites swept through the region and settled in Canaan. Over time they transitioned from a nomadic society to a stationary one, eventually building cities and populating the mountain regions. The Amorite wave was the last successful mass migration into the land until the coming of the Israelites.

The Amorites conquered the lightly populated mountains, but the existing Canaanite city-states that were built on the plains were under no threat: they were well fortified and well provisioned, and a nomadic society is seldom capable of capturing large, fortified settlements.

That the Egyptians tolerated the invasion without retaliation is meaningful. If the road system had been in any danger, or if Egyptian power had been seriously challenged, they would no doubt have marched against the Amorites. Whatever dominance the Amorites achieved was apparently not a significant threat to Egyptian control.

Abraham, throughout the time he was in Canaan, lived among the Amorites, interacting with them and using their services when needed:

> *"Then one who had escaped came and told Abram the Hebrew, for he dwelt by the Terebinth tree of Mamre the Amorite brother of Eshcol and brother of Aner, and they were allies with Abram."* (Genesis 14:13)

Some of the larger city-states in Canaan were Hazor, Joppa, Gaza, and Jericho. Abraham, on his way to rescue Lot after he had been carried off by the conquerors of Sodom and Gomorrah, must have passed by Hazor on his way to Dan. The leaders of Hazor (probably the Amorite capital) offered help to Abraham in what they must have considered a continuation of the war described in Genesis 14.

Abraham was not alone in his rescue operation. Based on what we read in Genesis 14:24, he led a much bigger army to confront the enemy north of Damascus:

> *" 'Except only what the young men have eaten, and the portion of the men who went with me: Aner Eshcol, and Mamre; let them take their portion.' "*

In light of Abraham's experience in Egypt and his interaction with Pharaoh (Genesis 12), he must have been well known in the land, since it was under Egyptian control and he himself was in a position of leadership. We can assume, therefore, that the clan of Abraham was acknowledged, respected, and integrated within the larger Amorite communities that occupied the hill country. The Biblical history of the Patriarchs often describes their interaction with these peoples.

On the other hand, Abraham was virtually unknown in the Canaanite cities of the valleys and coastal plains, and these cities do not figure in the Biblical narrative. This omission testifies to the prevalence of cultural differences and ingrained prejudices, and also to the inferior position of the mountain peoples. All of these things encouraged the Israelites to avoid interaction between themselves and the people of the coast. This bias is illustrated in Ezekiel 16:3:

> *"Thus says the Lord God to Jerusalem: 'Your birth and your nativity are from the land of Canaan; your father was an Amorite and your mother a Hittite.' "*

God, angry at the nation of Israel for its idolatry, reminds Jerusalem of her inferior past with a pointed reference to these two pagan nations. The Hittites and the Amorites were the two main civilizations inhabiting the area in and around Jerusalem before King David conquered it and established it as his capital.

Israel Returns to Canaan

Four hundred and thirty years in Egypt transformed the clan of Jacob into the nation of Israel. Of these years, the

Bible is mostly silent, and the tremendous changes that had taken place in Canaan during this time also go unrecorded in Scripture. When the Israelites entered the Promised Land, they found a Canaan vastly different from the land Jacob and his family had left behind four hundred years before.

For the first two centuries after Jacob migrated to Egypt, Canaan was relatively quiet. But the fifteenth through the fourteenth centuries B.C. brought great upheaval: almost simultaneously, a massive movement of nations – coming from all directions – collided in Canaan.

There is uncertainty regarding the exact date of the Israelite Exodus from Egypt. In two different places, the estimated time is mentioned: Jepthah, the judge, while dealing with the Ammonites, states that his forefathers came to the land some three hundred years earlier (Judges 11:26). Solomon marks the dedication of the Temple in Jerusalem as taking place 480 years after the Exodus (1 Kings 6:1).

Because the dates of Solomon's reign are known, a simple calculation results in a date of around 1440 B.C. for the Exodus. This is confusing when one tries to synchronize the Exodus with events in Egyptian annals that involve Canaan. For instance, the Egyptian chronicles tell us that around 1300 B.C. Seti I led the Egyptian army through Canaan. The Israelites' presence in the land is not mentioned (however, this does not prove their absence).

Several decades later, troops led by Pharaoh Mereneptah, stormed through the land. The name Israel is mentioned in relation to this campaign, which dates to around 1207 B.C.

The fact that ancient kingdoms sometimes neglected to mention failed military campaigns may be the reason that Egyptian annals do not mention Israel until 1207 B.C. – after all, what proud nation would want to admit what Exodus describes in chapter 14:23-28?

> *"The Egyptians pursued them, and all Pharaoh's horses and chariots and horsemen followed them into the sea. During the last watch of the night the LORD looked down from the pillar of fire and cloud at the Egyptian army and threw it into confusion. He made the wheels of their chariots come off so that they had difficulty driving. And the Egyptians said, 'Let's get away from the Israelites! The LORD is fighting for them against Egypt.' Then the LORD said to Moses, 'Stretch out your hand over the sea so that the waters may flow back over the Egyptians and their chariots and horsemen.' Moses stretched out his hand over the sea, and at daybreak the sea went back to its place. The Egyptians were fleeing towards it, and the LORD swept them into the sea. The water flowed back and covered the chariots and horsemen--the entire army of Pharaoh that had followed the Israelites into the sea. Not one of them survived."*

Canaan's political climate and the general mix of its population on the eve of the Israelite appearance are unknown, but we can assume that Israel's arrival was impossible to ignore. Reading the words that Rahab spoke to the men sent to spy out the land (Joshua 2:8-11), one senses the horror and fear that raced through the people as the Israelites poured in:

> *" 'I know that the LORD has given this land to you and that a great fear of you has fallen on us, so that all who live in this country are melting in fear because of you. We have heard how the LORD dried up the water of the Red Sea for you when you came out of Egypt, and what*

> *you did to Sihon and Og, the two kings of the Amorites east of the Jordan, whom you completely destroyed. When we heard of it, our hearts sank and everyone's courage failed because of you, for the LORD your God is God in heaven above and on the earth below.' "*

A few documents from Egyptian and other sources mention waves of nomadic tribes invading Canaan at this time, and Canaanite city-states were sending urgent messages to Egypt requesting military assistance. They refer to these invading tribes as the "Habiru." Whatever the exact course of events, by the twelfth & thirteenth centuries B.C., there were three or four major groups in Canaan.

The Israelites

A somewhat loose federation of tribes, the Israelites might not yet have considered themselves truly a nation, but they did share one religious center and worship the same God. They settled in the mountain regions of what became known in Biblical times as Galilee, Judea, and Samaria.

Following the death of Joshua, Israel's tribes lacked leadership, they were divided politically, and they were separated geographically. Whenever the pressure was intense, God would appoint a judge to attend the problem. However, none of the judges were considered a national leader.

The Philistines

The second group was the Philistines, relative newcomers in the land. The Philistines were a naval power that for unknown reasons were forced to leave their land on the Isle of Crete and settle on the coasts of Canaan. They were known as "The People of the Sea."

Theirs was a completely foreign culture to the others around them, but they possessed a clear superiority of weapons and warfare. They came into the land in a series of consecutive migrations. One wave successfully shattered the Hittite Empire, reducing it to a number of small impotent kingdoms. (Some Hittite refugees fled to the north of Israel, and became integrated into the culture of Canaan; e.g. Abraham purchased a burial cave from Ephron the Hittite in Genesis 23. Both he and Sarah were entombed there.)

The first wave of Philistines had sailed across the Mediterranean Sea, landed in the Nile Delta, and waged war with the Egyptians. The armies of Pharaoh Rameses III barely won the war, and the Egyptians wisely decided to recruit the Philistines by encouraging them to settle on the southern coast of Canaan and become allies of the Egyptian Empire.

Thus, the next two successive waves of Philistines arrived in Canaan and settled there with Egypt's blessing. They were based in five city-states that occupied both the southern coast and the lowland plains. Although they possessed superior weaponry and societal organization, the Philistines were severely outnumbered. Still, they soon dominated the land and sea trade that passed through Canaan.

The Canaanites

The third group that inhabited the land at this time consisted of the Canaanites, who lived in city-states that for the most part were built along the major trade routes. These Canaanite cities were heavily involved with the commerce moving along the highways. Due to their mutual interest in profitable trade, there was a degree of cooperation between the Canaanites and the Philistines.

The Arameans

The fourth group, not yet well established in the area, was the Arameans, later known as the Syrians. The Arameans originally came from central Asia. Over time they migrated across the Euphrates River, settling on her western banks. Eventually they would play a major role in the region's history for almost three centuries, but at this time they were a modest presence.

A Political Vacuum

Towards the end of these 800 years I have designated as the Canaanite Era, there was a political vacuum in the region due to the decline of Egypt, and the destruction of the Hittite empire.

During this era, Israel was still a tribal society divided by contradicting interests. In contrast, the Philistines and the Canaanite city-states were well organized and powerful; but this did not mean they maintained their dominance effortlessly.

With the decline of Egypt as a regional power, the Philistines no longer possessed a formidable ally and were compelled to preserve their fearsome reputation on their own. Eventually this led to their attempt to subdue the Israelites in order to establish their dominance over the region.

This is the context that led to the conflict between Israel and the Philistines which features so prominently in the books of

1st & 2nd Samuel. The battle at Eben Ezer, which resulted in the capture of the Ark, the destruction of Shiloh, and the routing of Israel's army, made it look as if the Philistines had won the war.

This concerned Israel's elders. They felt the nation needed a strong leader, someone who would go before them in battle and enhance Israel's reputation. This was the reasoning behind their demand to Samuel:

> *"All the elders of Israel gathered together and came to Samuel at Ramah. They said to him, 'You are old, and your sons do not walk in your ways; now appoint a king to lead us, such as all the other nations have.' " (Samuel 8:4-5)*

Samuel did not think this a good idea; God himself was their king. But the Lord, after telling Samuel to explain the "cost of a king" to the people (verses 10-18), said he would give them what they wanted. A youth named Saul

> *"an impressive young man without equal among the Israelites – a head taller than any of the others," (9:2)*

was anointed the first king of Israel.

3

The Kingdom
c. 1020-610 B.C.

The United Kingdom

Once Saul became king, he had to subdue the Philistines if he hoped to maintain his kingdom. For the next thirty years, the battle over the land was between the Philistines and Israelites. God gave Saul many victories, but He was not pleased with him, and decided to remove the kingdom from him and give it to someone else.

God chose David (1 Samuel 16), and David shows his courage and faith in front of the Israelite army in 1 Samuel 17:46-50 – his confrontation with Goliath.

> " *'This day the LORD will hand you over to me, and I'll strike you down and cut off your head. Today I will give the carcasses of the Philistine army to the birds of the air and the beasts of the earth, and the whole world will know that there is a God in Israel. All those gathered here will know that it is not by sword or spear that the LORD saves; for the battle is the LORD's, and he will give all of you into our hands.'*

As the Philistine moved closer to attack him, David ran quickly towards the battle line to meet him. Reaching into his bag and taking out a stone, he slung it and struck the Philistine on the forehead. The stone sank into his forehead, and he fell face down on the ground. So David triumphed over the Philistine with a sling and a stone; without a sword in his hand he struck down the Philistine and killed him."

The nation fell in love with David, a handsome young man whom the Bible describes as "a man after God's own heart." Saul originally befriended David, but later became suspicious of him and accused him of treachery. David had to flee Israel in fear for his life. He spent time in Philistine territory – able to convince them that because Saul wanted to kill him, he was their friend and an enemy of Israel.

Eventually Saul and his son Jonathan were killed in battle, and the Philistine victory over Israel seemed decided. Their intent was to set up a puppet king in Israel. This king would take orders from and serve the interests of the Philistines. David, having convinced the Philistines of his reliability, would have been the perfect choice, but he slipped out of Philistine territory, returned to Hebron, and reigned as king of Judah for seven years, until Saul's son Ish-Bosheth (who was ruling Israel) was killed.

Then, with the full approval of Israel's elders, David became king over all Israel, reuniting Judah with the other tribes. He conquered the Amorite city of Jebus in the heart of the hill country, and established it as his new capital – Jerusalem.

When David, in gratitude, asked God for permission to construct a house (the Temple) for Him, God denied his request, but said:

> *" 'When your days are over and you rest with your fathers, I will raise up your offspring to succeed you, who will come from your own body, and I will establish his kingdom. He is the one who will build a house for my Name, and I will establish the throne of his kingdom forever. I will be his father, and he shall be my son. When he does wrong, I will punish him with the rod of men, with floggings inflicted by men. But my love will never be taken away from him, as I took it away from Saul, whom I removed from before you. Your house and your kingdom shall endure forever before me; your throne shall be established for ever.' " (2 Samuel 7:12-16)*

Both Jew and Christian see this Scripture as God's promise to send the Messiah through King David's line.

Under King David, Israel seized the control that the Philistines had previously held over the region. David's power and influence spread, and nearby rulers soon established political contacts with Israel. These included the king of Hamath to the north, and the Phoenician kings of Tyre and Sidon.

The treaty between Israel and Sidon was mutually beneficial to both kingdoms. Israel had no desire for a navy but the Sidoneans had mastered the sea trade. They needed access to provisions – and a strong ally to protect their rear. It was a perfect match that lasted for centuries.

The success of David's reign and the frequent wars he conducted in the region expanded the circle of nations the Israelites came in contact with. King David would eventually subdue his foes and greatly extend Israel's borders.

These amazing victories were accomplished without iron chariots, without a professional army, and in a very short time. The nation of Israel had at last reached the borders of the land

God had promised to Abraham – from the Euphrates River in the north to the Brook of Egypt in the south.

David ruled for forty years. Despite his great successes, his throne was not secure. At least twice, open rebellion broke out. His son Absalom led the first rebellion. He was David's eldest surviving son, and the nominal heir; but God had told David that Solomon (his son by Bathsheba) would wear the crown. Absalom's revolt was quickly followed with one led by Sheba, the son of Bichri, of the tribe of Benjamin (Saul's tribe).

The nation at this time is described in the Bible as two groups: Judah and Israel. Sheba's revolt drew all but the tribe of Judah, and began with the cry "We have no part in David," emphasizing the breach between Judah and the rest of the tribes; the tension would continue to grow.

God protected David's throne, however, and by the time Solomon's reign began, Israel was well established as a kingdom. He inherited an empire without any powerful enemies, which made his reign notable not only for its great prosperity, but also for its peace and tranquility. Like his father, Solomon reigned for forty years. He was the first hereditary king of Israel.

In Solomon's time Israel was a powerhouse in international commerce, playing a major role in the region. Lucrative trade had translated into an overflowing treasury, allowing Solomon to make some enormous investments. For instance, he radically changed the nature of the army from light infantry (as it was in David's day) to one dependant on iron chariots. In doing so, Solomon was following the military models of the Egyptian and Hittite kingdoms.

The charioteers formed a new class of military elite. They owned land and other property and possessed political power and many class-related benefits. This was not popular with all of Israel. We can assume that most of the people who enjoyed the new benefits were from the king's tribe – the tribe of Judah – and that the gap between Judah and the rest of Israel continued to grow.

At the same time, power in the region was beginning to shift. Egypt was coming out of a long period of impotency, fueled by the rise of the Libyan Dynasty and the Pharaoh Shishak; Egypt sought to resume its dominance by inserting itself into local affairs. In an attempt against Israel, a relatively small-scale invasion by Egyptian troops allied with the Philistines had great success – reaching all the way to Gezer, only 35 miles from Jerusalem.

The building of the Temple and the massive complex containing Solomon's magnificent palace drained Israel's treasury and affected the economy. The previous trade agreement with the Phoenicians for building materials (in exchange for food) was no longer equitable. Solomon had to renegotiate, and in order to complete the construction, had to cede ownership of twenty cities to the King of Tyre.

Another major project that Solomon entered into was a joint venture with the Phoenicians to build a new fleet. Focusing all his interest and attention on such endeavors blinded Solomon to the changes taking place around his kingdom. For example, the Arameans on the northern border rebelled and broke free from Solomon's domination. The small kingdom of Edom also successfully rebelled. Losing control of these territories meant the loss of a large section of the main trade route and a significant loss in trade-related revenue.

Although we are not told in the Scriptures of any unrest or riots, we *are* told that God was unhappy with Solomon, who had turned to idolatry in his old age. God told him that because of this, he would take the kingdom from Solomon's heir – although not all of it (1 Kings 11:1-13):

> *" 'Yet I will not tear the whole kingdom from him, but will give him one tribe for the sake of David my servant and for the sake of Jerusalem, which I have chosen.' " (Verses 11-13)*

Because we know from history that this occurred, we might conclude that unrest and unhappiness was already brewing during Solomon's reign.

The last years of Solomon's life saw the loss of a great deal of the nation's territory, and with it, a decline in Israel's status. The dichotomy between Solomon's description as the world's wisest and wealthiest man, and the political and military weakness he eventually showed, is hard to explain, were it not for the fact that we can read of Solomon's personal failings and know that all men, the greatest of kings or the lowest of slaves, reap what they sow.

With his death the nation faced its greatest test so far, for there was now a challenger to the throne, the throne that God had said he would wrest from Solomon's heir.

The Divided Kingdom

Rehoboam, Solomon's son and the crown prince, was 41 years old when he convened the nation's leaders at Shechem for his inauguration (1 Kings 12). He apparently had no sense of potential crisis. To him it seemed a simple formality. But it was not just a technicality to elect the king. It was the right of the elders to give their consent, just as they had given it to his grandfather David. When the elders advised him to rule with compassion, he rejected their advice and took the advice of his young friends – to threaten to scourge the people. "All Israel" responded:

> *" 'What share do we have in David, what part in Jesse's son? To your tents, O Israel! Look after your own house, O David!' "(Verse 16)*

This event essentially marked the moment at which Israel became a divided kingdom. Judah was established as the Southern Kingdom, the only portion that God did not remove from Solomon's heir. It included the tribes of Judah and Benjamin. The Northern Kingdom retained the name of Israel and was comprised of the ten other tribes.

Within a few years, Pharaoh Shishak stormed into both Israel and Judah, determined to once again impose Egyptian control over the entire region. 2 Chronicles 12:2 tells us Shishak came because the people had been unfaithful to the Lord.

Fifty years of civil war followed the division of the monarchy. During these fifty years an unprecedented event took place: Asa, the king of Judah, bribed the Arameans to invade Israel's territory. His purpose was to create pressure on Israel – which was in the process of invading Judah – and force them to retreat. (While the Israelites and the Philistines had been fighting Israel's "War of Independence," the Arameans had been slowing amassing power and thus were in the position to offer meaningful help.)

The Assyrian Threat

Along with the growing power of the Arameans, the more serious threat of Assyrian domination loomed. For a time, King Ahab of Israel and King Jehoshaphat of Judah joined forces. Jehoshaphat's declaration ended the years of civil war and ushered in a short term of peace:

" 'I am as you are and my people as your people; we will be with you in the war.' "(1 Kings 22:4)

These longtime rivals were willing to set aside their animosity for a while and work together to halt the Assyrian advance. Even the Arameans joined the effort; the whole region was mobilized to wage war against the Assyrians and stop their westward encroachment. Ahab's marriage to Jezebel (a daughter of the Sidonean king) and the giving of his daughter Athaliah in marriage to Jehoram (the son of Jehoshaphat, king of Judah) were meant to strengthen the coalition.

In 858 B.C. a new king came to power in Assyria: Shalmaneser III. In his first year as king he led his army through Aramean land and into Phoenician territory. The Assyrians reached the Mediterranean Sea – and without any difficulty declared their victory over the region.

After recovering from the shock caused by the Assyrian advance, a coalition of twelve armies (from Egypt and from kingdoms west of the Euphrates) joined forces to confront the threat. Among the twelve kings of the coalition, was Ahab, the king of Israel. The epic battle took place at Karkar (in northern modern-day Syria) in 853 B.C.

Although the Assyrian forces did prevail, the conflict served to slow them down; but they returned to invade the land west of the Euphrates again and again, confronting the same coalition of kings. Eventually, in 841 B.C., the Northern Kingdom under Jehu, was forced to cede some of its territory to Assyria.

Aramea also had been weakened: Assyria had exerted massive pressure on the area and had almost destroyed the Aramean capital of Damascus. When Assyria's attention was diverted for a short time toward the emerging kingdom of Arrarat on its own northern border, King Jeroboam II was able to restore the boundaries of Israel somewhat by annexing Aramean territory:

> *"He restored the territory of Israel from the entrance of Hamat to the sea of Araban, according to the word of the Lord God of Israel." (2 Kings 14:25)*

This was the last time the Northern Kingdom of Israel experienced any great prosperity.

The long war between the Assyrian Empire and the coalition finally ended with a decisive Assyrian victory. Assyria moved on to subdue Egypt, the other strong power. Once again Israel stood in the way. There was no longer a strong Aramean empire to hide behind, and by allying themselves with Egypt, both Israel and Judah had made themselves enemies of Assyria.

Since Israel still controlled the main roads and the Assyrians' route to Egypt, it was attacked first. This assault in 732 B.C. led to the fall of the eastern parts of the kingdom – the mountains of Gilead. Some parts of Galilee were also torn away. The death toll was horrible, as we read in the book of the prophet Hosea:

> *"Therefore tumult shall arise among your people and all your fortresses shall be plundered as Salman plundered Beth Arbel in the day of battle, a mother dashed to pieces upon her children." (Hosea 10:14)*

In 722 B.C. the Assyrian army returned again. This time Egypt, not Israel, was its target. Israel's territory, however, still included a large portion of the international road system, and could jeopardize the Assyrian supply lines. Therefore Israel had to be destroyed.

Three years of siege commenced. Israel's capital city of Samaria suffered a terrible famine, finally falling in 721 B.C. This time, the Israelites were exiled to Assyria. The Bible tells us:

> *"Then the King of Assyria carried Israel away captive to Assyria." (2 Kings 18:11)*

The Bible is not very clear about the scale of the exile. Were all of the Israelites removed and the land left vacant? Does the exile mean that the tribes were "lost" as we refer today to the "ten lost tribes?" Most likely that was not the case; in later passages the Bible often mentions the tribal identities of people. Seven centuries later we are told that Paul was from the tribe of Benjamin; Hannah from the tribe of Asher.

The Bible also tells us that after the exile:

> *"Then the runners went throughout all Israel and Judah with the letters from the king and his leaders, and spoke according to the command of the king: 'children of Israel, return to the Lord God of Abraham, Isaac and Israel; then He will return to the remnant of you who have escaped from the hand of the kings of Assyria.' " (2 Chronicles 30:6)*

There are many scattered populations that claim descent from one or another of "the lost tribes." Historically, however, little is known of their specific fate.

The Assyrians took many captives: the aristocracy, the army, the clergy, and other influential leaders. Many Israelites still lived in Galilee and Samaria, but the Northern Kingdom as an independent entity came to an end. The kings of Judah (the

Southern Kingdom) would now consider themselves responsible for those Israelites who still lived in the land.

The Assyrian-Egyptian struggle had once again caught Judah between a rock and a hard place. The kings of Judah, a small, weak, and insignificant kingdom in the new order of things, had to wend their way carefully between the powers that dwelt on either side. Reading the Bible, one can sense the frustration of the prophet Isaiah as he encourages the king not to side with the Egyptians; but the king does not listen:

> *" 'Look now, you are depending on Egypt, that splintered reed of a staff, which pierces a man's hand and wounds him if he leans on it! Such is Pharaoh king of Egypt to all who depend on him.' " (Isaiah 36:6)*

The Assyrian army had to make sure that the route remained open as it marched through Judah toward Egypt. Rebellious Judah, unchallenged at the rear of the army, was too great a risk. Soon after the destruction of the Northern Kingdom of Israel (722-1 B.C.), the Assyrians attacked Judah.

Part of the Assyrian army climbed the mountains of Judea to lay siege around Jerusalem. Hastily, King Hezekiah executed two large-scale defense projects: a new wall was erected around the city and a water tunnel was built to bring water from the spring of Gihon (the main water source outside the walls) into Jerusalem to the pool of Siloam, so that sufficient fresh water could be obtained without leaving the city.

The Bible tells us that despite all these preparations, it was God who saved Jerusalem:

> *"And it came to pass on a certain night the angel of the Lord went out, and killed in the camp of the Assyrians*

> *one hundred and eighty five thousands; and when people arose in the early morning there were the corpses, all dead." (2 Kings 20:35)*

What remained of the Assyrian army withdrew.

Jerusalem survived the threat, but the rest of the country had suffered severe damage. The conquered cities were given to the Assyrian allies in the region – the hated Philistine kingdoms of Gaza and Akron – and Judah grew weaker yet and more vulnerable to her foes.

By 671 B.C. Assyria had conquered Egypt, but that conquest was short-lived. Having reached its zenith, Assyria itself was in decline. While the Assyrian army was engaged in war away from home, rising powers such as the kingdom of Babylon were flexing their muscles. For nearly a century Assyria survived assaults from neighboring countries. Finally in 612 B.C. the Babylonians conquered the Assyrian capital city of Nineveh – and Assyrian dominance was broken.

It was during the chaos of the Assyrian-Babylonian war that the Southern Kingdom of Judah, under King Josiah, enjoyed its last years of greatness. The newly ascendant Babylonian empire was still occupied with domestic matters when King Josiah annexed most of the former kingdom of Israel to his own territory.

Once again, the house of David was ruling over virtually all of Israel. But the Babylonians, about to claim their share of world history, headed south to conquer Egypt. Once again, Judah was in the way.

Meanwhile, Assyria, in a last attempt to save its empire and stand against the Babylonians, approached the Egyptians for help. In 616 B.C. an Egyptian army joined with the Assyrian army in fighting the Babylonians in Mesopotamia. Another Egyptian army marched out from the south to assist. This Egyptian force had been recently humiliated by an invasion of Scythians, who had turned back after Pharaoh Neco, on the throne for less than a year, paid a substantial ransom; the soldiers were anxious to prove themselves.

King Josiah, probably under orders from Babylon, tried to block these Egyptians as they headed north to Mesopotamia. He deployed his army on the plains of Megiddo and confidently met Pharaoh's army. But at the first skirmishes, even before the battle heated up, King Josiah was mortally wounded. His army dispersed, leaving Egypt to claim the victory.

Pharaoh Neco ordered that Jehoahaz (Josiah's son, who was crowned after his father's death), be removed after only three months on the throne and replaced by his brother Eliakim, whom the Pharaoh renamed "Jehoiakim," which means "He whom Jehovah has set up." God's reminder, perhaps, that He "sets up kings and deposes them."

Judah was now under Egyptian rule, and Israel had already ceased to exist. The promise that was the Davidic dynasty had all but disappeared.

4

Removed and Returned
c. 610 – 510 B.C.

For a few years, the battleground between Egypt and Babylon was to the far north. But soon after the Babylonians secured Assyria, they crossed the Euphrates, determined to confront the Egyptian army further south.

Their first attempt in 607 B.C. was a failure. The Egyptian stronghold in Carchemish (an ancient city on the Euphrates River, northeast of Aleppo in present-day Syria) held. Years of unrest followed, as the armies of Babylon and Egypt continued to collide.

You are that Head of Gold (Daniel 2:38)

In 605 B.C. the Babylonian crown prince Nebuchadnezzar defeated the Egyptians in a decisive battle at Carchemish, and the backbone of the Egyptian army was broken. The Egyptian defeat echoes in Jeremiah 46:24:

> *"The daughter of Egypt shall be ashamed, she shall be delivered into the hands of the people of the north."*

The Babylonian forces amassed in Judah for their final attack against Egypt. This effectively caused Judah to lose its last vestige of independence.

In Jeremiah 36:9 we read:

> *"Now it came to pass in the fifth year of Johoiakim the son of Josiah, king of Judah in the ninth month that they proclaimed a fast before the Lord to all the people in Jerusalem and to all the people that came from the cities of Judah to Jerusalem."*

Proclaiming a fast was an act of unusual significance and demonstrated great fear and distress. In the Babylonian annals we find the reason for concern – the Babylonian army had conquered Ashkelon, which had sided with Egypt, and no doubt was now advancing on Jerusalem.

Jehoiakim had every reason to be concerned by the Babylonian advance. After submitting to the king of Babylon three years earlier, he had reversed his position and allied Judah with Egypt instead. Furthermore, God had already said that the Babylonians would conquer the nation. With a Babylonian victory, punishment was inevitable.

If he had any hope that an Egyptian expeditionary force might yet save Judah, 2 Kings 24:7 reveals the true picture:

> *"And the king of Egypt did not come out of his land anymore, for the king of Babylon had taken all that belonged to the king of Egypt from the brook of Egypt to the river Euphrates."*

The stress and tension in Judea are well reflected in the Scriptures. While the official policy was to side with Egypt, the prophet

Jeremiah had long counseled submission to Babylon (Jeremiah 21 and 27).

Jerusalem was conquered by Babylon in 597 B.C. and the first of several exiles took place. Some thirty thousand people, the cream of Judean society – including most of the professional army and the prophet Ezekiel – were removed. After reigning only one hundred days, King Jehoiachin (who had succeeded his father Jehoiakim in approximately 599 B.C.) went into captivity with the rest of the nobility. A new ruler was appointed by Babylon and installed at Jerusalem – King Zedekiah.

Zedekiah soon revolted. Quickly, the Babylonian king threw all of his army at this relatively weak adversary. Tenacious Jerusalem held on for nearly two years before it fell, but it was at great cost. The city, the Temple included, was destroyed and its houses burned down. Many more captives were exiled to Babylon.

However, in various places around the country, a Judean remnant was left behind. With Babylonian blessing, these settlers stayed in the land to ensure that the cities, vineyards, farmlands, etc. did not become desolate and ruined through lack of use.

This situation only lasted a few years because the Babylonian-appointed governor was murdered:

> *"But it happened in the seventh month that Ishmael the son of Nethaniah, the son of Elishama, of the royal family, came with ten men and struck and killed Gedaliah. The Jews as well as the Chaldeans (Babylonians) that were with him at Mizpah. And all the people small and great and the captains of the armies arose and went to Egypt; for they were afraid of the Chaldeans."* (2 Kings 25:25)

Unlike Assyria, Babylon did not settle people from other countries in a newly conquered area. However, a slow yet steady infiltration of Edomites from across the Jordan valley did come and settle in the almost deserted land. When Israel returned after the captivity, these foreigners, who would heavily resist Judah's resettlement, had comfortably and tenaciously filled the void.

Nebuchadnezzar, the Babylonian king who conquered Jerusalem, had many of the Jewish royalty and those of aristocratic birth trained to serve in his government. The prophet Daniel appears to have served the kings of Babylon throughout the entire captivity. We first see him as a young man being trained for Nebuchadnezzar's court, and we last see him announcing the end of Babylon to the current monarch, as he interprets "the handwriting on the wall."

The books of Daniel, Jeremiah, and Ezekiel all take place during the period of the captivity. They are excellent sources of information about this time, particularly as they were written from different locales. Daniel was a government official in Babylon, Ezekiel apparently lived in rural Babylon, and Jeremiah, still in the land after the third exile, was taken with other remaining Jews to Egypt, where he continued to prophesy to the nation.

Nebuchadnezzar's Dream

In the Book of Daniel, in Chapter 2, Daniel interprets a dream for King Nebuchadnezzar of Babylon. It involved a statue that was made of five different materials. The head was of gold, chest and arms of silver, belly and thighs of bronze, legs of iron, and feet partly of iron and partly of baked clay (Daniel 2:31-45). It is an amazing prophecy that lines out the future of the Middle East for the next six hundred years.

> " *This was the dream, and now we will interpret it to the king. ...You are that head of gold. After you,*

> *another kingdom will rise, inferior to yours. Next, a third kingdom, one of bronze, will rule over the whole earth. Finally, there will be a fourth kingdom, strong as iron- for iron breaks and smashes everything- and as iron breaks things to pieces, so it will crush and break all the others. Just as you saw that the feet and toes were partly of baked clay and partly of iron, so this will be a divided kingdom; yet it will have some of the strength of iron in it, even as you saw iron mixed with clay. As the toes were partly iron and partly clay, so this kingdom will be partly strong and partly brittle.... 'The great God has shown the king what will take place in the future. The dream is true and the interpretation is trustworthy.' "*

Biblical interpretation of this passage is fairly uniform; the first kingdom is Babylonia; the second is the Medo-Persian Empire, then the Greek Empire, and finally the Roman Empire. Each of these kingdoms was the master of the land of Israel for a time.

In chapter 7 of Daniel, the kingdoms are spoken of as four animals: a lion, a bear, a leopard, and a "terrifying beast." In chapter 8, we are also told of a ruler who would desecrate the temple (Antiochus in 168 B.C.) and that the temple would be re-consecrated (as it was by Judas Maccabeus in 165 B.C.).

As Daniel had said earlier in Chapter 2:

> *" 'Praise be to the name of God for ever and ever; wisdom and power are his. He changes times and seasons; he sets up kings and deposes them. He gives wisdom to the wise and knowledge to the discerning. He reveals deep and hidden things; he knows what lies in darkness, and light dwells with him.' " (Daniel 2:20-22)*

Daniel knew God had the determined the fall of the nation, had determined the length of its captivity, and he would also determine its future.

After the murder of the Babylonian Governor Gedaliah, the remnant of Judah – including the prophet Jeremiah – fled to Egypt and left the land virtually deserted of Jews.

We have few sources that allow us to picture the effect of the war and the Babylonian exile on the land itself. We do know that unlike the Assyrians, the Babylonians did not purposely resettle a conquered area, and they established no official colonies in Israel; the land became a blank canvas.

On their own initiative, neighboring peoples began to infiltrate the mostly empty Judean territory. From the coast, the Philistines took over the lowland. From across the Jordan River, the Edomites fled from the Nabateans into the lush and still useful land. The Samaritans, who considering themselves Jews and were the only body of people with some Jewish ancestry, expanded their holdings towards the south into what had been the land inhabited by the tribe of Benjamin. Still, during the years of the exile, most of Judea, especially the area around Jerusalem, remained barely populated.

The Medo-Persians

" 'After you, another kingdom will rise, inferior to yours.' "
(Daniel 2:39)

The Persians, under Cyrus the Great, overthrew Babylon in approximately 539 B.C. and assumed control of all its territories. Thus Judea became once again a border country, replaying its role as a bridgehead in the ensuing Persian effort to subdue Egypt.

The local population was crucial to this attempt. What Cyrus and his successors needed were loyal and grateful subjects on the outskirts of the empire. This is how to regard Cyrus' declaration permitting the restoration of Judea (described in the Bible in 2 Chronicles 36:22-23 and Ezra 1:2-3) from a historical perspective – the Persians had learned that their multiethnic and multinational empire generally submitted peacefully when it was allowed to practice religious freedom.

However, the prophet Isaiah (around a hundred years before the proclamation – Cyrus was not yet even born) prophesied of God's intent to bring the Jews back to their homeland after the Babylonian Captivity; this is how to understand Cyrus' decree from a Biblical perspective:

> *"[God,] Who says of Cyrus, 'He is my shepherd and will accomplish all that I please'; he will say of Jerusalem, 'Let it be rebuilt,' and of the temple, 'Let its foundations be laid.' (Isaiah 44:28)*
>
> *'I will raise up Cyrus in my righteousness: I will make all his ways straight. He will rebuild my city and set my exiles free, but not for a price or reward, says the LORD Almighty.' " (Isaiah 45:13)*

Cyrus' proclamation was considered by the exiled Jews to be a divine sign, the fulfillment of the prophecies spoken of in the book of Isaiah. In the Bible, God had described the Babylonian captivity as punishment for sin, specifically the sin of abandoning the God of Israel through the worship of idols. God had said the Jews would remain in exile until they were purged of this sin. Apparently the lesson was well learned. After the Babylonian Captivity, Israel never again practiced idolatry as a nation. After fifty years, God allowed them to return home.

The first wave of returnees to Zion numbered around fifty thousand (Ezra 2:64). The entire Jewish community in Babylon was excited about the proclamation. However, side by side with the opportunity to return to their homeland and rebuild their temple, was the knowledge that they were leaving behind a comfortable existence to venture into the unknown. Many of the exiles had prospered in Babylon, and the Jewish community there was well respected. The Jews had been able to maintain a surprising degree of cultural and social autonomy. So, despite the excitement and enthusiasm engendered by the decree, when the time came to return to Judea, many chose to remain in Babylon.

Persia had no intention of restoring Judah's political position. Cyrus' declaration had only to do with the reconstruction of the temple so that the people would once again have their center of worship. Although instigated by royal command and funded through the empire's treasury, the project faced many obstacles from the beginning. One can only assume how the foreigners living in Israel (having appropriated Judean houses and lands) felt when they heard of the decree.

The Samaritans no doubt feared that their position as legitimate successors to the Jews would be seriously undermined by the Jews' resettlement in the land. The Edumeans (the Edomites), expelled from their country across the Jordan, were also deeply concerned. Too many people in the area, including the Persian governors who held offices in the land, had too much to lose.

Jerusalem still lay in ruins from the destruction of decades before. (Nehemiah tells us that the walls had been broken down and the gates destroyed by fire.)

From the very beginning, conflict surfaced between the returnees and the locals; the Samaritans even expected to take part in the Temple's restoration. They were denied, although this must have surprised them, since they considered themselves of the same faith; but during the exile in Babylon, the Jews had returned to the undiluted tenets of the Mosaic Law. To the newly Orthodox Israelites, Samaritans were Gentiles and unclean; their faith was not strictly that of Moses. They could not possibly help in the temple reconstruction. The Samaritans, not being aware of this fundamental change in the Jewish mindset, were deeply offended.

Whatever the nature of the opposition, the pressure bore fruit and work halted on the reconstruction of the temple. For nearly twenty years, the altar that had been erected on the Temple Mount (soon after the first returning Jews arrived) had to serve as the focal point of worship until the Second Temple was completed.

With the unrest that followed Cyrus' death, Persian dominance in the region was undermined by Egypt and by other local forces. It wasn't until Darius, the new Persian emperor, reunified the empire that stability returned and conditions allowed the work on the temple to resume.

The prophets of this era, Haggai and Zechariah, repeatedly encouraged the people to complete the work. Their new aspirations were of a political nature as well, as reflected in the words of the prophet Haggai:

> *" 'I will shake heaven and earth. I will overthrow the throne of kingdoms; I will destroy the strength of the gentile kingdoms. I will overthrow the chariots and those who ride in them.... 'In that day,' says the Lord of hosts, 'I will take you Zerubbabel my servant, the son of*

> *Shealtiel,' says the Lord, 'and will make you like a signet ring; for I have chosen you,' says the Lord of hosts.' " (Haggai 2:22-23)*

The rebuilt temple is known historically as "Zerubbabel's Temple." With its completion in 515 B.C., Israel believed that a new era had commenced: God's wrath and punishment were over; the new temple heralded reconciliation between God and his people.

The limited number of Jews in the land brought another wave of reform many years later, this time conducted by Nehemiah. The walls of Jerusalem were rebuilt, but not without opposition; after "Sanballat, the Arabs, the Ammonites" and others plotted to fight against Israel, Nehemiah wrote:

> *"From that day on, half of my men did the work, while the other half were equipped with spears, shields, bows and armor. The officers posted themselves behind all the people of Judah who were building the wall. Those who carried materials did their work with one hand and held a weapon in the other, and each of the builders wore his sword at his side as he worked. But the man who sounded the trumpet stayed with me. Then I said to the nobles, the officials and the rest of the people, 'The work is extensive and spread out, and we are widely separated from each other along the wall. Wherever you hear the sound of the trumpet, join us there. Our God will fight for us!' So we continued the work with half the men holding spears, from the first light of dawn till the stars came out." (Nehemiah 4:16-21)*

Side by side with the city's fortification by Nehemiah, came vast spiritual and social reforms under Ezra.

Ezra was given a letter by the Persian authorities that acknowledged the Torah as an official religious code and authorized Ezra to run the nation's life under its rules and customs. The support of the royal Persian court encouraged many in Babylon to join Ezra on his journey to Jerusalem.

Those who did not join him nevertheless supported their relatives in Judea. Their desire to help the community in Jerusalem was the outcome of deep concern, a commitment that illustrated that the Jews in Babylon were in solidarity with the Judeans. (A similar situation exists today with the state of Israel and the world, especially American Jewry.)

Ezra and Nehemiah, both devout Jews acting as Persian officials, came to Judea nearly a century after Cyrus had made his declaration. Those Jews already there were comfortable in their status and some adjustments were inevitable. For instance, the settlers had been practicing intermarriage with local pagan women.

Nehemiah, equipped with imperial authority, instigated reforms that were not completely embraced by the local leadership. As long as he stayed in Judea his decrees were kept, but upon Nehemiah's departure the high priest permitted intermarriage and tried to integrate the Samaritans with the Jews. This succeeded so well that for over a century, until the Greek conquest of the land, the Samaritans held high positions in every field: public, economic, and religious.

By the end of the Persian era, Israel was a land that had seen many changes. The Jews who had returned from Babylon dominated a small area with Jerusalem in its center, Hebron to the south, the Shefelah (lowland) to the west, Samaria to the north, and the Sea of Salt on the east.

Neighboring nations had invaded former Judean territory: the Philistines reoccupied some of their forefathers' land along the

Mediterranean coast. The Phoenicians built colonies along the coast and on the main crossroads.

Israel was still not confident in its ability as a nation to fend off the re-introduction of pagan worship. The Jews may have tried to isolate themselves and only interact in a minimal way with their neighbors; however, they were constantly exposed to other cultures, and in order to develop a national presence in the area, it was necessary to interact with those cultures.

The changes in the land's demographics and the fact that the Persians had replaced the Babylonians were not that important to daily existence. The religious and public life remained much the same. Whether under Egyptian or Persian control, the Jews found the means to protect their culture and survive among the nations.

5

Various Overlords
c. 510 – 167 B.C.

" 'Next, a third kingdom, one of bronze, will rule over the whole earth.' " (Daniel 2:40)

As the Persian Empire continued its westward expansion, it collided with the Greek world at the beginning of the 5th century B.C.

This was more than just another war between two powers motivated by the ancient greed to conquer land and dominate trade. It was the titanic clash of two different worldviews.

The Greek world and its views on democracy and individual worth elevated freedom and celebrated the human spirit and man's creativity. The Greeks hated any system that hinted at tyranny, and the social structure of the Greek world was different from any other system that existed at the time. The idea that every man and woman had a unique role and a voice in public life was revolutionary to other nations.

By challenging the right of a ruler to be an absolute monarch and to treat his subjects as he pleased, the Greek mindset contradicted the current social order and threatened the Persian Empire just as successfully as an advancing army.

Persia's collision with the Greeks was a shocking experience to the empire: its army was defeated again and again by a small country with limited resources and manpower.

The Greek viewpoint made this possible. Even for the average Greek foot soldier, the war was his personal concern. Because Greek society celebrated the individual, the Greek soldier fought not merely for a king but for his own personal freedom. He was willing to sacrifice in order to preserve it. That motivation and that spirit were keen advantages in warfare and produced an army that did not easily surrender or accept defeat.

The Greeks also introduced a highly effective fighting formation known as a phalanx: soldiers arranged in tight formation, carrying spears and protected by their overlapping shields. During the fifth and fourth centuries B.C., the Greeks and Persians collided a number of times. Neither posted a decisive victory, but the reputation of the Greek army continued to grow and neighboring powers learned to beware.

These encounters gave the Greeks a place of prominence in the ancient world. As the Persian Empire weakened during the fourth century, and gradually surrendered its dominant position, the Greek world was able to impose itself into the very heart of the Levant.

During the Greco-Persian wars, soldiers from numerous small and independent Greek kingdoms and city-states (polis) were melded into one power that not only stopped the Persian offensive, but led a counterattack deep into Asia Minor. Eventually, under Alexander the Great, Greek authority extended all the way to India.

Under the command of Alexander, in less than ten years the Greco-Macedonian forces spread Greek culture throughout the lands they conquered. This was the stated goal of the young Macedonian – to bring the whole world under Grecian influence.

Deteriorating conditions in Greece (a lack of fertile land and an exploding population) encouraged many citizens to seek a living elsewhere. Often, Greek civilians followed the trail of the army.

Alexander also gave land to army veterans, guaranteeing the establishment of colonies in remote regions and the promotion of the Greek ideal. These veterans brought their families along, exerting an immediate cultural effect upon their surroundings.

The Greeks Change the Landscape of Israel

The Greeks faced a unique problem when they began to establish new settlements in Israel – the local cities and towns in many places were built upon manmade hills, called Tels, which could only accommodate a small number of people.

The Tels were the natural outcome of the practice of layering a new city atop the ruins of an older one. This was done in order to stay close to the already established water source, but it had a built-in problem: each new layer had to be somewhat smaller then the previous one; in order to have a well-anchored wall for the new city, engineers were forced to build its foundation several feet in from the location of the most recent wall.

In other words, the first city that was built on the site encompassed the largest area, and the area of each subsequent city became smaller and smaller.

The Greeks, with their tendency toward large public buildings, required many more square feet for their cities than the top of a Tel could provide. Through advanced engineering, water engineering in particular, the Greeks changed the appearance of cities in Israel.

These new cities, with public facilities and large entertainment areas including theaters and stadiums, were built not on top of, but surrounding the ancient Tels. In most cases the original Tel, now enclosed within a large, sprawling metropolis, became the elevated location of a temple dedicated to the local Greek god.

The House of Thalami and the House of Seleucus

Alexander the Great died in June of 323 B.C. in Babylon. With his death so far from home, confusion and disorder soon caused the disintegration of his empire. Two decades of chaos and civil war, during which lands were conquered and lost and agreements signed and violated, ended with a reassignment of power in the Middle East: the house of Thalami ruled Egypt, the house of Seleucus ruled in Asia, and the house of Antigonus reigned over Greece and Macedonia.

Once again, Israel was between a rock and a hard place – wedged between the houses of Thalami and Seleucus. Both kingdoms practiced and promoted Greek culture, and by their intrusive presence, they intensified the Hellenization of the entire region. For over a hundred years, Israel was the victim of a fierce tug-of-war between the two powers.

Despite five major wars waged on Israel's soil between the two, the house of Thalami (Egypt) was able to maintain its hold over Israel into the third century B.C.

From a Jewish standpoint, the main challenge during that time was not which kingdom held sway; it was how to respond to the rapidly spreading Greek influence.

The Greek culture promoted a new concept of the relationship between God and man. It also introduced a different understanding of the fixed order of things – assuming the position of man at and as the center of the universe.

Placing man at the center of all existence led to the promotion of a luxurious lifestyle as the supreme goal of life. The beauty of the human body was worshiped, resulting in an explosion of fine arts dedicated to celebrating its form. Debate replaced doctrine. Philosophers and philosophy reigned supreme, sometimes with the intent not to further knowledge, but to further the reputation of the speaker while casting doubt on the viewpoint of the opponent.

Greek culture also offered something which was very attractive to the common man: every individual, regardless of his wealth and social status was by default a valued member of society – not merely a means of tax revenue.

This idea, coupled with the Greek culture's presentation of man as the center of all creation, offered a tempting alternative to the simple, faith-based, class-driven Jewish lifestyle. The nation's leadership had to label the Greek influence as dangerous, without alienating those Jews who were attracted to it.

On the whole, the other peoples living in the land welcomed the Greek influence. The new system seemed a boon to ordinary citizens, with its guarantee of more freedom and a greater voice in government.

The response of the Jewish nation to the new culture was more varied. The lower classes could not afford to embrace it at the level that was most attractive. The upper classes of Jewish society, though, possessed the necessary resources to experience what the culture offered.

They tried to adopt some elements of it, reasoning that there were no laws that forbade the enjoyment of life. However, the pantheon of Greek gods was ignored. Greek statues were forbidden according to the second commandment. Participation in the popular Greek games and attendance at the bathhouses were perennially debated but never forbidden.

It is difficult to discern how deeply rooted the Greek philosophy was among the Jews of this age. The Jewish population was growing at this time, both through the birthrate and by Jews returning after the Diaspora. This newly minted Jewish society found itself struggling with the influx of Greek culture: How much was too much?

The Greek way inherently brought tension into Jewish life. Things strange and uncomfortable were replacing the familiar parameters of Jewish tradition. However, because of the varied backgrounds of the new Jewish society, the nation was already developing an internal breach; it utilized the Greek influence in expanding that breach but would not have required it.

Antiochus III & Thalami IV

Almost simultaneously in 223 B.C., two young and ambitious kings came to power – Antiochus III in Seleucia (also referred to as Syria) and Thalami IV in Egypt. In a few years, Antiochus led his first invasion into the Egyptian territory of Israel (in 218 B.C).

As the Syrian army advanced through Israel, it was stopped near Rafah, on the northeastern edges of the Sinai Peninsula. This first confrontation between Antiochus III and Thalami IV ended with a victory for Thalami's as Antiochus was forced to retreat.

Returning to his capital, Antiochus planned another campaign to Israel and once again, the Syrians penetrated deep into Egyptian territory – as far as the gates of Gaza. When the Egyptian army advanced to rescue Gaza, the Syrians pulled back to the foot of Mount Hermon. The two armies met again in 200 B.C. and this time the Syrians were victorious.

Israel, after 120 years of Egyptian domination, now came under the control of Antiochus and the Syrians. The Jewish population of Israel apparently accepted this new master willingly. They had provisioned the Syrian army as it had marched by Jewish towns en route to Egypt. Because of this, the Syrian king rewarded the Jews – especially those in Jerusalem – by exempting them from various taxes, by providing acceptable animals for the temple sacrifices, and by forbidding the importation of unclean animals into Jerusalem. Antiochus also issued a decree guaranteeing religious freedom.

It seemed that after a century of war on Israel's soil, both tranquility and prosperity were within reach. Little changed in Israel following the Syrian victory, for its new masters practiced the same Greek disciplines and lifestyle. As long as circumstances were normal, tension was minimal between the two cultures.

The Seeds of Revolt are Sown

While Syria and Egypt were focused on their mutual struggle, neither paid much attention to what had happened across the Aegean Sea. The Roman army, defeating the Macedonians, had crossed the Bosporus and Roman boots stood for the first time on Asian soil, in an area controlled by Syria.

When Antiochus III and his troops confronted the Roman army in the city of Magnesia, in 188 B.C., the Syrians lost the battle and were forced to evacuate Asia Minor. This was a severe blow: valuable territory was forfeited, the number of troops that could now be mobilized was significantly smaller, and the revenues associated with the land were also lost.

Antiochus IV replaced his father in 175 B.C. He inherited an inconvenient situation. Reforms were needed in the empire to promote loyalty and obedience – and vast amounts of money were required to save the empire and stop Roman expansion.

Antiochus IV was determined to Hellenize his entire kingdom. In order to accomplish this, he decided to rescind the promises of religious freedom that his father had made.

In most places this would have had little effect. The replacement gods had different names, but the things supposedly controlled by them (weather, fertility, war, etc.) were the same. Most people in the region could thus easily and willingly identify with the new gods. However, the Jews would never accept integration into the pagan world through a forced exchange of deities.

Along with the new religious reforms came cultural reforms. The type of government in the subject countries was changed to a "polis," the common government of Greek city-states. This change completed the formal Hellenization of the empire. Sources indicate that the Jews were more flexible with the political structure – the polis form of government – than with the religious changes forced on them by the Syrian authorities.

The government also decided to tax the incomes of the various temples in order to fill the treasury. The Jews found this idea abhorrent. The money that was given at the Temple was consecrated to God and dedicated for temple use only; it was not to be used for any other purpose. This government interference in the religious arena served to encourage renewed unrest.

Back in 175 B.C. when Antiochus IV had assumed power, Jason, from the Jewish priestly line, offered him a large sum of money to be appointed high priest and to introduce the new polis form of government in Jerusalem. The king granted Jason's request.

A few years later in 172 B.C., another member of the priesthood, Menelaus, bribed the king with a larger sum of money than what Jason had offered. (Due to a shortage in his own resources, Menelaus took money from the Temple's treasury to pay this bribe. This blatant embezzlement did not disqualify him from becoming the high priest.) Jason was removed from his position, and Jerusalem was split between two camps.

In 169 B.C. When Jason's supporters heard the rumor that Antiochus IV had died in battle, they attacked Jerusalem. Antiochus, very much alive, pulled out of Egypt and marched his forces north to suppress the revolt.

Upon arriving in Jerusalem, in what must have been a calculated insult designed to demoralize the Jews, he plundered the Temple and desecrated the altar by ordering a pig to be sacrificed upon it.

Before the revolt, the high priest had been considered the ruler of the Jewish people. Now, determined to abase the Jews and further subjugate them, Antiochus IV neutralized the high priest's power by appointing his own governor to maintain law and order.

In another attempt to control the situation and stop the riots, Antiochus also issued new religious decrees. His main objective was to craft a united, homogeneous empire. By forbidding circumcision, the study of the Torah, and the keeping of the Sabbath and Jewish feast days, the Syrian king hoped to forcibly but finally assimilate the Jews into the Greek culture, including the mandatory worship of Greek gods.

Years of internal debate and disagreement fell away in the face of these new restrictions. The masses, the lower strata of the Jewish society, led the revolt.

It is possible that some of the Jewish leaders had previously led Antiochus to believe that the majority of the Jewish people would accept these decrees peacefully, for it is clear that the resistance and the rebellion that followed took the Syrians by surprise. It was not a coincidence that the focal point of the revolt was Modin, a small town in the lowland, rather than Jerusalem – a cosmopolitan and definitely more liberal city.

A family from the village of Modin, the Hasmoneans, led by Mattathias from the priestly division of "Yehoyariv," led the insurrection, known today as the Hasmonean Revolt. In 167 B.C., fleeing to the mountains of Gofna in the land of Benjamin, the rebels waged three years of guerilla warfare against the Syrian army.

Mattathias of Modin died early in the conflict, as did his sons Eleazer and John. Three other sons – Judas, Jonathan, and Simon – figured prominently in the revolt and the years that followed.

Judas carried the nickname Maccabeus, or The Hammerer. He is considered a master strategist and a charismatic general, whose leadership contributed significantly to the success of the rebellion. History shows him a fine commander and able soldier. In fact, the revolt is known to many not as the Hasmonean Revolt, but as the Maccabean Revolt, in recognition of his vital role.

Between 166 and 164 B.C. the Hasmoneans, led by Judas, repeatedly defeated the Syrian armies. The rebels gained strength and confidence with every victory. Eventually, the Judean army took Jerusalem. The Temple was formally cleansed from the defilement it had suffered under Antiochus IV, and the sacrificial system was restored. The people celebrated this achievement with a great festival; Jews today still commemorate this event through the feast of Hanukkah.

6

The Rise and Fall of the Hasmoneans c. 166 – 63 B.C.

In Syria, Antiochus IV had died and the situation degenerated into civil war. The Syrians, looking for allies in case any other nations sought to take advantage of their instability, abolished the existing religious decrees in Israel and gave the Jews a new autonomy. Many Jews had only been concerned about religious freedom; once this was restored, the Hasmonean revolt lost much of its momentum. When a new Syrian army marched against Judea, only few Jews joined the rebel army; The Jewish army was defeated and Judas Maccabeus was killed. Judas' successor, his brother Jonathan, had to flee to the wilderness and resort once again to guerilla warfare.

In an unexpected turn of events, the political instability in Syria became the means by which Jonathan was able to come out of hiding and openly lead his people: Alexander Balas, a challenger to the Syrian throne, offered Jonathan the position of high priest in an effort to gain Jewish support. Demetrius, another royal hopeful, countered Balas by offering Jonathan military control of Palestine and the governorship of Jerusalem. Jonathan accepted Balas, and thus founded the Hasmonean priesthood.

The Syrian unrest that continued throughout Jonathan's life allowed him to strengthen both Judea and his own position. He served through the reigns of three Seleucid kings, finally dying when a Seleucid general, during a period of instability, seized and executed him.

A Monarchy Once Again

Despite Jonathan's success, it was his brother Simon who founded the Hasmonean kingdom and guided Israel toward renewed independence. When Jonathan died, Simon was recognized as his successor. Simon's diplomacy and skillful leadership enabled Judea to continue to profit from the domestic troubles in Syria.

Previously, as the governor of the coastal regions, Simon had invited Jews from other parts of the country to settle there, effectively conditioning the territory for future annexation. The port of Joppa, the gate to commerce with other countries, lay within this region. Fortresses were also erected in the desert, guarding the inland highways.

Eventually, the elders of the nation formally recognized Simon as Judea's leader, and an assembly was convened in Jerusalem in August of 140 B.C. Its main objective was to determine the form of government that the nation would assume. It was decided that Simon's authority would include all matters of state, the high priesthood, and command of the army, and that the office would be hereditary. Four hundred and forty years after the Temple was destroyed and the Davidic monarchy came to an end, men of Jewish descent would rule their own homeland.

The elders' endorsement of Simon was in essence a declaration of monarchy, although he was denied the title of king. Instead, Simon's title was probably "The Head of the Jews." Two other important manifestations of power were also withheld: the ability to legislate and the right to judge. These remained in the hands of the nation's elders.

Although, the kingdom was secure – accepted by the Syrians, and bound by treaties with both Rome and Egypt – Syria continued to regard Judea as a strategic asset for its own purposes. During the reign of the Judean king Hyrcanus 1st, the Syrian king Antiochus Sidetes attacked and conquered Judea. For a few years, Judea lost its independence, and Hyrcanus was forced to join with Syria in its war against Persia. Only the death of Antiochus Sidetes in battle (129 B.C.) restored Judea's independence.

Despite such interruptions, Hyrcanus conquered Judea's neighbors and expanded its borders. He also instituted mass religious conversions in the annexed countries. In Edumea, as in other subdued nations, citizens were given the choice to convert to Judaism or to leave the area. Those in the larger Hellenized towns preferred to retain their culture and religion, and they left Edumea rather than convert; but most people accepted their new masters and were integrated into Jewish society. This absorption was so complete that eventually a family of Edumean converts would ascend to the Jewish throne – the line of Herod.

Samaria was next. From the time of the divided monarchy, the Samaritans had considered themselves Jewish – but they had their own temple (on Mount Gerizim) and considered it more sacred than the one in Jerusalem. They were conquered, their temple destroyed, and they came under Hasmonean rule.

Following Hyrcanus' reign, Galilee was annexed (104-103 B.C.) and its inhabitants forcibly converted. By the end of the second century B.C. – the beginning of Alexander Janaeus' reign – all of the land west of the Jordan River and some of the eastern regions were under Jewish dominion.

The Hasmonean kingdom reached its peak under Alexander Janaeus (his Jewish name was Jonathan). During the twenty-seven years of his reign (103-76 B.C.), the kingdom experienced both defeat and victory as he attacked several rivals: the coastal cities of Acre and Gaza, the Hellenic cities of the Trans-Jordan, and the land of the Nabateans (they had settled Edumea after the Edumeans had migrated into Israel during the Babylonian Exile).

Civil Unrest

Despite his ability to expand the kingdom, Janeaus lost the support of the elders and the national assembly by his attempts to appropriate titles and powers denied him by the agreement his grandfather Simon had signed forty years earlier. He was already the high priest; the leaders resented his persistent desire to gain the title of king, for fusing the religious and secular functions in the hands of one individual was unthinkable to the Jews.

Constant warfare and heavy loss of life and property soon brought open revolt among Janeaus' subjects. The farmers, in provisioning the troops and the rest of the nation, carried the burdens of the ongoing expansion while the upper classes enjoyed most of the benefits.

Violence erupted into civil war. Seven years of chaos followed (90-83 B.C.) tearing the country apart. The Hasmonean kingdom was weakened, though Janeaus continued on the throne. In an act that was to have severe repercussions, he decided not to renew Judea's treaty with Rome (signed by Judas Maccabeus in 161 B.C. and renewed by all other successors).

Janeaus was strongly supported by the Sadducees, a sect that seems to have developed at the time of the Hasmonean revolt. The Sadducees were primarily of the priestly class: wealthy individuals of high social standing. Josephus, writing later, said:

"They only gain the well-to-do; they have not the people on their side." The Sadducees warmly embraced the Hellenistic culture.

The other primary sect, the Pharisees, disavowed all things Hellenistic and favored the total retention of Jewish culture. They became almost "a law unto themselves" in their quest to separate from outside influence, and had great influence over the common people. The two sects epitomized the widening breach between the Jewish people.

Janeaus died in battle and was replaced by his wife, Shlomzion. She, realizing many people disapproved of her late husband's ties with the Sadducees, aligned herself with the Pharisees. This meant that the kingdom began to depart from the Hellenic lifestyle and move back to a more Jewish form of life and government.

When Shlomzion died in 67 B.C. her two sons (Aristobulus and Hyrcanus 2nd) fought over the throne. Focused on their own interests, they engaged in a civilly destructive war, even as the avaricious Roman general Pompey crouched at the borders of the kingdom. Incredibly, the two aspirants to the throne agreed to ask Pompey to settle their dispute.

This desire of each (to draw such a powerful ally to their side) was only natural. However, it was an open invitation to Rome to involve itself in Jewish national affairs. When the two brothers took their case to Pompey, it was the first step in the demise of the kingdom: the Roman Empire recognized Judea as powerful – therefore a potential risk to Rome's plans for the region. In addition, the Hasmonean practice of conquering Greek cities and converting their inhabitants was a threat to Rome's own culture.

> *" 'Finally, there will be a fourth kingdom, strong as iron -- for iron breaks and smashes everything--and as iron breaks things to pieces, so it will crush and break all the*

> *others. Just as you saw that the feet and toes were partly of baked clay and partly of iron, so this will be a divided kingdom; yet it will have some of the strength of iron in it, even as you saw iron mixed with clay. As the toes were partly iron and partly clay, so this kingdom will be partly strong and partly brittle. And just as you saw the iron mixed with baked clay, so the people will be a mixture and will not remain united, any more than iron mixes with clay.' " (Daniel 2:40-43)*

Pompey decided in favor of Hyrcanus – but only after the Roman army marched to Jerusalem and laid siege to the city, causing thousands of casualties among its defenders and bringing down the Hasmonean kingdom. In 63 B.C., eighty years of independence came to an end. Twenty centuries would pass before the Jews would live again in the land as an independent nation.

Death Throes

In the matter of only a few years a nation that had dominated a vast area, with an overwhelming Jewish majority, lost its independence. Many of its people, those forced by the Hasmoneans to abandon Greek culture, now became enemies of the Jews.

Until the Roman conquest, most people in the Hasmonean kingdom were Jews. Some were second-generation converts, often with still-lingering ties to their forefathers' pagan ways of life. Others were more recent converts who zealously practiced Judaism as a means of displaying loyalty. However, for the average Greek Hasmonean subject – forced to convert to Judaism when conquered – the Romans appeared as saviors.

In the Trans-Jordan, which was a recently conquered area still in the process of conversion at the time of the Hasmonean defeat, anti-Jewish sentiments were strong. The new Roman occupiers, with their stated position as protectors of the Greek culture, encouraged many of the converts to abandon the Jewish way of life recently forced upon them. They were invited to return to their pagan gods, this time with Roman support and protection.

The Jews found themselves in an impossible situation. Overnight their authority disintegrated, and in many areas they were outnumbered. Under Roman approval, the formerly subject Greek cities could claim autonomy and seek revenge. Hostility grew between Jews and Greeks.

The Jews had not completely given up on their dream of an independent kingdom. With the memory of the Jewish victory over the Syrians less than a century before, some Jews regarded this new bondage as an invitation to try for independence; but the desire to resist the Roman occupation was by no means a national one. Many Jews, mainly the lower classes who had never enjoyed any prominence or economic relief under the Hasmoneans, did not take part in the resistance.

Thus the breach in Jewish society surfaced again – this time in a new form: the following years were typified by a constant and bitter struggle, but only a portion of the nation figured in it – the Hasmoneans and their supporters. For nearly two decades, Hasmonean princes recruited thousands of followers to wage war against Rome. Time and again they were defeated. The Hasmoneans had much to lose – they included the former royal family and the Jewish upper class (the Sadducees) – and they persevered valiantly against the Romans. But the rest of the nation – the Pharisees and the lower classes – were not involved in the struggle.

Without unified support, the rebellion faded away. Twenty long years of resistance ended with devastating results: the elite of Jewish society were almost totally destroyed. The heavy losses – tens of thousands of men – created a huge vacuum: politically, economically, and militarily, many of the nation's potential leaders were gone.

Religious leaders (men who had previously been oppressed by the former Hasmonean regime) moved in to fill the void. They now took on vital roles as the secular aspects of the peoples' lives came under their power.

Not surprisingly, these leaders had one main interest: the nation's religious freedom. As long as spiritual freedom was guaranteed, they were willing to compromise the political status of Judea and accept cultural changes. In fact, much of the nation was willing to ignore the lack of political independence for the sake of religious freedom. However, especially among the Galileans, many still considered political freedom to be their main goal; such men kept the dream of freedom alive.

7

The Edumean Rulers c. 60 B.C. – 10 A.D.

With Jewish resistance effectively at an end, Rome now turned its attention to stabilizing the region. Troublesome Judea was situated on Rome's easternmost border. With the Persians across that border and only miles away, the Roman Empire needed a faithful populace that would share pro-Roman sentiments and serve as a protection for Rome until Judea became a fully integrated and loyal Roman province.

To accomplish this, the empire formed the Decapolis –the league of ten cities. These cities, all inhabited by people of Greek descent, were ruled and formed after the manner of the Greco-Roman polis. Until the Roman culture was accepted in Judea, and a loyal king governed the province, the Decapolis would serve to keep the Jews from forming an effective alliance with Persia against Rome.

With the Hasmonean dynasty virtually destroyed, it was only natural that other Jews sought to appropriate that power for their own. The Romans, utilizing the proven "divide and conquer" strategy, carefully watched these opportunists to see whom would best serve their own purposes. They realized that placing someone of Hasmonean descent in a leadership position would keep the flame of Jewish nationalism burning – something they wanted to prevent. Therefore, Rome looked for someone who was not a Hasmonean and who would be committed to Rome – a person of unquestionable skills, but a man who would place his own agenda above a national one. No less important was the fact that such a figure had to be accepted, or at least tolerated, by all the ethnic groups in Judea – Jews, Greeks, and Samaritans. A family of Edumeans began to play a key role in Judean politics.

The Line of Herod

When conquered peoples had been forced by the Hasmoneans to convert or leave their homelands, those that had chosen to convert gained the opportunity to participate in local politics and, in various ways, to obtain substantial influence. The most outstanding example of this was the family of Antipater the Edumean. Antipater, the first of the line, was a Jewish convert who embraced the Roman culture as superior and thus was able, when Rome became his master, to attain a high and powerful position.

Antipater co-ruled with Hyrcanus 2nd, but in fact held most of the authority. Supported by the Romans, he had several unique opportunities to prove his loyalty to his new masters. He commanded an army that rescued Julius Caesar in Egypt and participated in other Roman campaigns. He was favored by Caesar himself, who eventually rewarded Antipater by appointing him as governor of Judea. To intensify his power in matters of state, and with Roman approval, he placed two of his sons in positions of great influence: his son Fazzael was appointed governor of Jerusalem; he named another son, Herod, as governor of Galilee (47 B.C.).

The death of Caesar (he was murdered March 15, 44 B.C.) and the resulting unrest created confusion around the empire.

The instability in Rome was felt in Judea as well, but with Mark Anthony as ruler of the East and at temporary peace with his future rival Octavian, the situation in Judea soon stabilized.

However, the Hasmonean dynasty was not yet totally erased and the legitimate heir, Antigonus, saw the insecure political situation as his chance to reinstate the monarchy and seize control. He arrived in Rome – demanding the position that he felt was legally his.

When his petition was denied by Rome, he turned to Persia, Rome's bitter enemy, to seek support for his attempt to claim the kingdom. The Judean governor Antipater was poisoned. His two sons, Herod and Fazzael, revenged his death by executing thousands of people.

The civil war in Rome and the anti-Roman sentiments in Judea were powerful incentives to Persia, which was always on the alert for an opportunity to invade Roman territory. The Persians attacked in 40 B.C. as Antigonus advanced towards Jerusalem. The city was taken and Herod and Fazzael fled; the Hasmonean prince Antigonus was crowned king of Judea.

The family of Antipater did not give up. With the death of his brother Fazzael, Herod left his family behind in Edumea and set off to Rome to seek the help of the Senate in restoring him to office in Judea. The Roman leaders Anthony and Octavian listened carefully to Herod's appeal. They realized that if Judea remained in enemy hands, the empire's land contact with Egypt would be jeopardized and the flow of grain to Rome might be cut off. They offered assistance.

A special session of the Senate confirmed Herod as king of Judea. To emphasis Rome's support, parts of Samaria and West Edumea were annexed to Herod's territory. The agreement was affirmed by depositing in Jupiter's temple the document detailing the decision. Herod, standing between Anthony and Octavian at a far-off pagan altar, was recognized by Rome as Judea's legitimate king.

In Judea, the news was received with contempt. If there was any debate about Herod's loyalty, the ceremony in Jupiter's temple highlighted the nature of that loyalty. Herod, it was soon proved, would viciously revenge the death of his brother and meet with murder the loyalty shown to Antigonus.

The Roman recognition of Herod as king was only the first step in reclaiming Judea for the empire. It took three years, numerous battles, and the death of Joseph, another of Herod's brothers, before Jerusalem was conquered and Antigonus, the last of the Hasmonean princes to hold power, was deposed and executed.

To undermine any remaining Hasmonean influence, Herod installed someone from outside of the country to take over the position of high priest. He also turned against the remaining Hasmonean supporters. Thousands were killed, including most of the members of the ruling council, the Sanhedrin. By the end of 37 B.C. Herod was the absolute monarch of Judea, terrorizing his subjects and commencing a reign that would be represented by thirty-three years of fierce domination.

Herod's appointment to the monarchy stripped the Jews of their national identity: the king was not even Jewish, let alone from the house of David. Their culture was being deliberately undermined. Furthermore, the priesthood was corrupt because the high priest was not from the tribe of Levi.

With Herod's reign, the Roman lifestyle was resolutely established in Judea. It was no longer a foreign discipline embraced only by the leading classes. Now it was the preferred way of life. It was, from Herod's perspective, a faithful imitation of what he saw and learned in Rome.

Once the civil war in Rome was over – with Octavian defeating Mark Anthony in the battle of Actium in 30 B.C. –

stability returned to Judea. Herod was able to dedicate himself to solidifying his hold on the monarchy and developing his territory.

Although he had to pay heavy taxes to the Roman Empire, the riches Herod was able to accumulate provided ample funding for numerous ambitious building projects, most of which involved religious or civic improvements. In fact, Herod is credited with the completion of several large and splendid construction projects in the region, and his reign is considered one of the greatest in history for such efforts.

Despite his civic enhancements, many of Herod's subjects despised him. To them, he was "The Edumean dog." To others he was more acceptable: they could tolerate a king who admired and imitated the Greco Roman life since he was also somewhat sensitive to the Jews' needs – even to the point of financing the construction of a new temple in Jerusalem. (The existing "Zerubbabel's Temple" dated from the time of the rebuilding of Jerusalem after the Babylonian Captivity, and had undergone no major improvements since then. It was apparently a singularly unimpressive building: the exiles old enough to remember the splendor of the Temple of Solomon had wept as its modest foundations were laid.)

Others appreciated the economic prosperity of his reign. The sources of Herod's wealth had filled up the treasury: from the "Sea of Salt," salt and sugar (date honey) were exported to Rome. From the mountains of Judea and Samaria came wine and olive oil. As reward for his excellent service to Rome, Herod was allowed to take over the lucrative trade of incense, spices, and perfumes coming from Arabia. The hordes of Jewish pilgrims (coming from every corner of the Roman and Persian empires to celebrate the feasts in Jerusalem) also represented a major source of income.

As long as Herod was in power and supported by the Romans, the ethnic, political, and social tensions within Judea were buried. It was a time of intermission. The old Jewish rivalries didn't disappear, however, and many waited, knowing that peace would not last forever. The Greeks, Jews, and Samaritans who lived under Herod's rule were anticipating the end of his reign and preparing for it.

Herod dominated his subjects ruthlessly and this allowed him to maintain the peace in his kingdom, which brought him imperial gratitude and support. But he feared assassination and intrigue so much that he single-handedly destroyed much of his own family. By his death in the year 4 B.C., some of his wives and most of his sons were dead by his own hands, victims of his paranoia. During the last years of his reign, ill and worn down, he lost much of his influence. On his deathbed, in an attempt to prevent his subjects from celebrating his demise, he ordered the execution of the entire Sanhedrin (an order that apparently was not obeyed).

Riots broke out soon after his death, in several places at the same time. Part of the army, stationed in Edumea, and parts of Jerusalem fell into the hands of rebels. The local commander, Sabinus, was unable to suppress the riots and sent for help. Varus, the Roman governor of Syria, amassed a significant force from neighboring nations and stormed Galilee – leaving thousands of casualties in his wake.

In Rome, Caesar Augustus delayed his approval of Herod's will until the civil unrest died down. Then, Herod's kingdom was divided into three smaller territories: Archelaus, Herod's oldest son, was appointed governor of Judea, Samaria, and Edumea (The region south of Jerusalem). However, the title "King" was denied him.

Antipas, another son, was made the ruler of Galilee and the "Perea," (The eastern side of the River Jordan) even though the two properties were not adjacent. Philipus, the youngest son, was appointed king of the upper Jordan valley, the Golan, and Bashan. Several royal estates were given to Herod's sister Salome.

After ten years in power, Archelaus was exiled to Gaul and in 6 A.D. Judea was designated a third class Roman Province, ruled by a Roman governor who himself was answerable to the Syrian governor. For the first time, Jews in Israel were governed directly by the Roman Empire and its representatives, with no local ruler to represent them and protect local interests.

These Roman governors, most of them of low status and without many resources, brutally exploited their powers. The Roman yoke grew heavier yet.

8

The Great Revolt
c. 10 – 70 A.D.

Judea's next sixty years were marked by a steady deterioration in its relationship with Rome. Tensions mounted as the Roman procurators in cities with heavily mixed populations sided with the Greeks. The preferred Roman policy seemed to be one of continual provocation against the Jews. Frustrated, many Jews found ways to retaliate, and thus invited further Roman oppression.

When the emperor Caligula ordered his image to be installed at Jerusalem, in the Temple's Holy of Holies, the passions of the Jews were inflamed. This intended defilement of the Temple might have drawn the entire Jewish population into open aggression against Rome, were it not for the deft maneuverings of King Herod Agrippa (in Rome at the time), which forestalled this ill-conceived plan.

The last golden age of Judea took place during this time. During his relatively short reign, Agrippa recalled the greatness of Herod I. However, unlike his Edumean grandfather, Agrippa had Jewish blood and therefore enjoyed a respect among the Jews that Herod I never received. He was also politically astute, enjoying the favor of Rome during Caligula's reign as well as that of his successor, Claudius.

Despite this favor, his reign lasted only seven years. The New Testament book of Acts tells us that Herod Agrippa died suddenly and violently after accepting shouted praise from the people of Tyre and Sidon:

> *"On the appointed day Herod, wearing his royal robes, sat on his throne and delivered a public address to the people. They shouted, 'This is the voice of a god, not of a man.' Immediately, because Herod did not give praise to God, an angel of the Lord struck him down, and he was eaten by worms and died." (Acts 12:21-23)*

Josephus writes in confirmation of this:

> *"A severe pain also arose in his belly, and began in a most violent manner. He therefore looked upon his friends, and said, 'I, whom you call a god, am commanded presently to depart this life; while Providence thus reproves the lying words you just now said to me; and I, who was by you called immortal, am immediately to be hurried away by death. But I am bound to accept of what Providence allots, as it pleases God; for we have by no means lived ill, but in a splendid and happy manner.' When he said this, his pain was become violent. Accordingly he was carried into the palace, and the rumor went abroad every where, that he would certainly die in a little time. … Now the king rested in a high chamber, and as he saw them below lying prostrate on the ground, he could not himself forbear weeping. And when he had been quite worn out by the pain in his belly for five days, he departed this life, being in the fifty-fourth year of his age, and in the seventh year of his reign" (Antiquities 19:8)*

Once again, Roman procurators were sent to maintain order, and Jewish loyalty to the Roman Empire became suspect: Jews lived throughout the empire; If the Judean Jews revolted, could those in Rome be trusted – or would they side with their brothers in Judea? The many Jews in Persia were an additional worry. If war broke out with the Jews, the enemy would be well represented at Judea's vulnerable eastern border.

Rekindled Hope

The Jewish desire had always been to jealously guard their culture. No matter where they lived, they sought to form their own separate society within the established one. This often drew resentment from those around them – resentment also fueled by the Jews' ongoing and undisguised desire for a return to national sovereignty. Because of the Jewish nationalistic mindset, many historians would argue that peaceable Jewish existence in the Roman Empire could never have been achieved.

As the Roman Empire expanded through conquest, most of its subject nations adjusted to the natural role of the conquered – submission, compromise, and eventual absorption. The Jews, however, through the promises of their scriptures, expected deliverance.

They were waiting for a promised redeemer who would restore Jewish sovereignty and Israel's supremacy in world affairs. This hope kept the Jews from ever submitting totally to Rome. (This hope of a conquering king was the reason many Jews rejected the claims of Jesus Christ as their Messiah, for he did not fit their expectations of a powerful worldly monarch and national Savior.)

Over decades of Roman occupation, the Jews had inevitably moved from fierce resistance to partial acceptance of Roman rule.

However, some always watched for the opportunity to revolt. Such enduring discontent kept the flames of national resistance burning, most noticeably in the repeatedly futile attempts by Galilean Zealots to drive out the Romans.

Not everyone in Israel was equally avid for freedom. Many wealthy Jews were more assimilated into the Greek culture than their less affluent countrymen; the unhappy commoners, unable to retaliate effectively against Rome, often directed their animosity toward the pro-Roman upper classes and the Jewish aristocracy.

Finally, in 66 A.D. several events combined to encourage a general revolt. First, the reign of the current Roman emperor, Nero, was ineffectual. While his tenure had begun with promise, after several years of dissipation and cruel intrigue he had little support (by 68 A.D. he was dead by his own hand). Secondly, the Roman army had been gnawed on by Persia a few years earlier and remained in a weakened state.

In addition, a wave of unrest had swept through the empire, leaving that same army to spend their remaining strength on frequent uprisings in Britain, in Gaul, and along the German border. While there was no evident consensus for an organized revolt, the opportunity was made attractive by the prevailing circumstances, and the Jewish commoners responded with enthusiasm.

The existing Jewish leadership at first shunned the revolt and tried to maintain Roman law and order with the help of Agrippa II, the king of Galilee. However, they quickly lost control over Jerusalem, which was the focal point of the unrest. Amazingly, in what may have been a desire to retain their powerful positions if the revolt succeeded, the leaders eventually abandoned attempts to suppress the revolt and assumed control of it instead.

Two hundred years before, dedicated Jewish rebels had wrested control of their homeland from Syria and re-established an independent Jewish kingdom. The new rebels looked for a replay of that historic event, seeing themselves as another generation of Jewish heroes. The atmosphere in Judea became one of hope – hope that the Jews, with the aid of the Persian Empire and the advantage represented by the general unrest, could successfully throw off the Roman oppression.

The fire of rebellion had first been kindled in one of the mixed cities – where the tensions between the Jews and the Greeks had slowly increased over the years of Roman occupation.

The spark was a domestic conflict over a pathway to the synagogue in Caesarea. Some Greeks had blocked the path on the Sabbath, effectively barring the Jews from their place of worship. The Roman authorities sided with the Greeks, and this led to violence in Caesarea, followed by massive riots all over Israel.

In Jerusalem, the daily offering for the sack of the Roman Emperor (Jewish acknowledgment of Roman sovereignty) was stopped. A company of Galilean zealots captured the desert fort of Masada. Since the local Roman troops could no longer maintain law and order, the governor of Syria, Cestius Galus, marched the 12th Roman legion toward Jerusalem, intent upon quelling the insurrection.

The Zealots, the group behind the revolt, rose to the occasion. The masses poured into Jerusalem to confront the Roman soldiers, and the battle raged inside and outside the city's walls. As the conflict ebbed, thousands of dead soldiers lay crumpled on the hills, punctuating the defeat of the Roman army. With cries of victory and the captured banner of the 12th Roman legion held high, the triumphant rebels gathered in Jerusalem.

As significant as this victory was, the Zealots could not escape the revenge of the Roman army. It was expected that retaliation for Galus' defeat would be sharp and swift. An effort was made to fortify strategic locations in Galilee, as well as to enlist the support of non-Jews – without which the whole venture would be in vain. The Zealots' chances for ongoing success were also hindered by the continued lack of a national consensus and the fact that Agrippa II, the Jewish king of Upper Galilee, was loyal to the Roman Empire.

While the Zealots hurried with their preparations for defense, the Roman army began its march: sixty thousand Roman troops, led by the famed general Vespasian, were on their way to Israel.

The Zealots' greatest asset was the intense religious and national zeal of their fellow Jews, and fierce battles erupted around some of the Jewish strongholds in Galilee. However, because of a lack of weapons and disciplined military training, this great dedication was not enough to best the Romans. Most Galilean cities opened their gates and welcomed the soldiers. Advancing in friendly territory with access to food and other provisions, the Roman army sped inland and went on to conquer one fortress after another. Town after town in Galilee and on the Golan mountains fell to the Roman assault.

With Galilee well in hand, Vespasian sent his troops by land and by sea along the coastline of the Mediterranean to the port city of Joppa. By destroying the Jewish naval force and capturing the town, the road to the interior lay wide open. The Romans' next objective was to totally isolate Jerusalem – the heartbeat of the rebels' zeal.

While the Roman army was clearing southern Judea of rebels, disturbing news arrived from home: the emperor Nero was descending into madness. Galba, the governor of Spain, supported by the governor of Portugal, had proclaimed himself emperor. One after the other, challengers fought over the empire. Galba was soon replaced by Otto, who was replaced three months later by Vitalius. The year of 68 A.D. is known as "the year of the four Caesars."

In Judea, Vespasian brought the war to an abrupt halt. Proclaimed as emperor by the eastern legions, he headed back toward Rome to seize the throne for himself. He appointed his son Titus as commander of the troops that would remain in Judea.

Since the situation in Rome was unclear and military help might be needed closer to home, the Roman army evacuated the portions of Judea they had conquered and encamped near the harbor cities of Caesarea and Alexandria, awaiting word from Vespasian.

For several months, with the Roman army away from Jerusalem and withdrawing from other parts of Israel, it seemed as if the war had ended, but with no specific outcome. The vagueness of the situation and the pause in hostilities with the Roman army intensified domestic tension among the Jews. Once again the Zealots and the aristocracy were at each other's throats. Instead of using the lull to work together and craft a national government that would arrange for the defense of Jerusalem, each group did whatever was in its power to undermine the other's authority.

In December of 68 A.D., after defeating the army of Vitalius, Vespasian became Rome's new emperor. He then moved quickly and decisively to end the conflict in Judea once and for all.

Titus deployed his four legions and auxiliary forces around Jerusalem. Ramps were built against the city walls and war machines were constructed. The first full-scale attack came from the north. Jerusalem's outer wall was breached, and Roman soldiers poured into the Antonia fortress, a strategic military location north of the Temple.

Fierce resistance stemmed the Roman flood at the walls of the fortress. But Titus, probably in a desire to save Roman lives, decided to starve the city instead of pressing an offensive attack. Jerusalem was encircled and provisions coming into the city were cut off.

Horrifyingly, as supplies dwindled within the city, the civil war continued on a new footing – the limited food and water was fought over by the slowly starving men, women, and children. Titus knew that no matter what came first – surrender or starvation – Jerusalem was his.

As the defenders weakened, Titus again attacked the Antonia fortress and the Temple Mount. In late July (the 9th of Av in the Jewish calendar), Roman troops penetrated the Temple courtyard; they entered the Temple only to find that in a last desperate act, the priests had set it on fire.

The Temple, the manifestation of Jewish national and religious existence, was aflame. With those flames, the newest vision of Jewish freedom fell to ashes. A month later, the rest of the city fell, and the Great Revolt was over.

A decorative stone frieze from the period, The Arch of Titus, depicts Roman soldiers carrying off the Temple's rich interior furnishings as the spoils of war. Josephus tells us that the price of gold fell by half once the incalculably valuable plunder was melted down and put into circulation.

Within a short time after the conquest of Jerusalem, the entire city was razed, including the Temple. The massive blocks of beautiful white lime stone that had been used in its construction were carted off from the Temple Mount and used in other buildings. It is said that rulers from the Muslim Umayyad dynasty and the Crusader period utilized the stones from the Temple in their own palaces.

"As he was leaving the temple, one of his disciples said to him, 'Look, Teacher! What massive stones! What magnificent buildings!'

> *'Do you see all these great buildings?' replied Jesus. 'Not one stone here will be left on another; every one will be thrown down.' "* (Mark 13:1-2)

Soon the area where the magnificent building had stood was no more than a desolate stretch of stone pavement, giving no hint at all of the glory that had once filled it.

9

After the Great Revolt c. 70 A.D. – 300 A.D.

The price of the revolt was dear: hundreds of thousands dead, a devastated and forfeit land, and the Holy Temple defiled, its majestic façade now blackened and forlorn. Pockets of resistance were still holding on (Masada, Herodion and Mecharus), but the revolt was effectively over.

Nineteen centuries would pass before once again the Jews would be an ethnic majority in Israel. Nineteen centuries in which the Jewish people were scattered among the nations: longing, dreaming and praying to return to Zion. It was clear that such a time would come. After all, God had promised his people:

> *"For I will take you from among the nations, gather you out of all countries, and bring you into your own land." (Ezekiel 36:24).*

For the Jews in the first century A.D, the hope of immediate freedom was replaced by the need for patience, and for a renewed faith that their God keeps his promises.

After the revolt, Judea began to be governed by a proconsul rather than a procurator. Proconsuls were generally men of higher status in the Roman administration, and this change reflected Rome's recognition of Judea's importance as a strategic border province. A Roman legion was deployed permanently in Jerusalem.

New colonies were established in Judea to tighten the Roman vise. Non-military retaliation crippled the Jewish economy: the estates of the wealthy were confiscated; a heavy burden of taxation was imposed, and rural Jews worked their fields no longer as landowners, but as mere tenants.

A Revised Form of Worship

With the loss of the Temple, the sacrificial system ceased. With the cessation of the sacrificial system, the priesthood faded away. Faithful Jews could no longer participate in Temple worship, could no longer bring animals to the priests for the required blood sacrifices, and could no longer bring the firstfruits of their harvests as offerings before the Lord.

The religious men, the leading rabbis, knew this did not mean the people were no longer required to worship God, so they sought to offer alternatives. In effect, they reinvented Judaism. The religious heart of the nation, the Temple, was replaced by local meeting places (synagogues). Lacking the ability to fulfill the sacrificial and ritual requirements of the law, the law instead was scrutinized and commentaried until for many, the commentaries superseded the law. Jewish religious life became dedicated to scholarship. The public, social, and religious lives were now centered in the synagogue instead of the Temple, under the tutelage of rabbis rather than under the ministry of priests.

As just another Roman province, the land of Israel lost its genetic identification with the Jewish people. No longer was there an unbroken bond between "the history of the Jews" and "the history of the land." Many other civilizations would appear and leave their mark. Over several centuries, diverse religions proclaimed the land "holy," and men fought and died in the defense of their creeds. These same creeds still detonate controversy in Israel today.

The revolt left a dark scar on the nation's collective memory. The desolated villages, the ruins, and the death toll were supposed to teach the Jews a lesson: this is the punishment for rebellion.

However, even such a costly defeat could not erase Jewish nationalism, and many worked afterward to restore what had been damaged. Land that had been confiscated by the Romans was redeemed by money sent by Jews of the Diaspora. Houses were rebuilt, and once again the soil was coaxed into sharing its riches.

Some five centuries earlier, the nation had acknowledged the Babylonian Exile as God's punishment for their disobedience and idolatry. During the exile, the nation repented and began again to submit itself to God. Men dedicated themselves to the study of the Law. When God allowed the nation to return to Jerusalem, it was seen as a fresh start.

It was hard for the Jews of the Great Revolt to find a spiritual reason for their defeat. They could not see the loss as punishment for sin, and blamed it instead on the lack of unity resulting from the divisiveness among the various sects in society. Therefore, the Sanhedrin, along with the rabbis, worked together to unite the people. By promoting reconciliation, the Sanhedrin and other leaders hoped to provide the glue that could hold Israel together.

After several decades, the Roman authorities began to show more tolerance toward the Jews in Judea. Another legion was posted there, and with two legions in the little province it seemed that tranquility was guaranteed. Under the surface though, the rebel spirit never died. With the ruined Temple as an enduring reminder of what they had lost, sooner or later another attempt would be made to cast off the Roman yoke.

The Bar-Kochba Revolt

Unfortunately, historical sources do not identify the catalyst for the Bar-Kochba revolt. It might have been the emperor Hadrian's intention to build a pagan temple on the Temple Mount. Another possibility was his decree prohibiting circumcision. The exact reason is unknown.

Why is it called the Bar-Kochba Revolt? A Jewish sage of the time, Rabbi Akiva, apparently used a man named Simon Bar-Kosba to rally the Jews. By altering his name to Bar-Kochba (which means "Son of a Star") and quoting Numbers 24:17-18, Akiva promoted him as the Messianic warlord of Israel:

> *"I see him, but not now; I behold him, but not near. A star will come out of Jacob; a scepter will rise out of Israel. He will crush the foreheads of Moab, the skulls of all the sons of Sheth. Edom will be conquered; Seir, his enemy, will be conquered, but Israel will grow strong."*

Although an effort was made to recruit Jewish Christians for the revolt, they did not participate. This was mostly due to the fact that Simon Bar-Kochba was portrayed as a Messiah; since their own allegiance was to Yeshua – Jesus Christ – Jewish Christians were not interested in taking part in what would essentially be a religious uprising, with Bar-Kochba as a Messianic figurehead.

Nevertheless, the revolt commenced – more unified and better organized than past efforts. Learning from experience, the rebels practiced guerilla warfare. Caves and hiding places were excavated in the mountains of Jerusalem and the Shefelah (the lowland); arsenals were equipped with weapons, and food was cached in subterranean locations known only to the rebels.

The Roman historian Dio Casius mentions that Jewish blacksmiths, forging swords for the Roman army, deliberately manufactured some with defects, knowing that the Romans would reject them. Thus many fine swords became available to the rebels.

This time, it took the Romans three years (132-135) to overpower the Jews. Six legions participated in the war, together with many auxiliary forces. There were no open battles between the two armies, however. The Roman general sent from Britain (Julius Severus) flushed the rebels from their hiding places as they were discovered, and gradually the rebels were pushed back south of Jerusalem to Beitar, the capital of the revolt. After a long siege the city was captured and the war ended.

Dio Casius states that nine hundred and eighty Jewish villages were destroyed and nearly six hundred thousand people were killed during the conflict, but most Jewish and non-Jewish sources are virtually silent concerning the Bar-Kochba Revolt. Without reliable historical sources to supply details, one must rely on fragments of information, such as these: The 22nd legion, which had been sent to Judea from Egypt, was removed from the list of Roman legions after the revolt, leading one to conclude that the legion suffered great losses and was forced to disband. Also, Hadrian's letter to the Senate describing the victory did not contain the traditional referral to the condition of his troops: "I and my troops are well." This is circumstantial evidence: however, it does seem to indicate that the victory came at a great price to Rome and that the Jewish rebels acquitted themselves well.

After the defeat, Simon Bar-Kochba was exposed as a false Messiah, and rabbinical writers began to refer to him as Simon Bar-Kozeba – Son of the Lie.

The Romans began to express their anger against the rebels in creative ways. Imperial decrees were enacted that seemed to have humiliation as their main objective – Jews were prohibited from entering the holy city of Jerusalem, which had been deliberately paganized and given a new name: "Ilia Capitalina." The teaching of the Torah and the ordaining of rabbis were prohibited, and Jews were forbidden to wear prayer shawls or exhibit other manifestations of the Jewish faith. The area began to be referred to as "Palestine," a name derived from "Philistine." To have their homeland named after this ancient adversary was a pointed insult to every Jew.

The aftermath of the Bar Kochba Revolt was much harsher than that of the Great Revolt. It was in fact a war of annihilation. Judea was devastated in such a way that generating a livelihood from the soil was impossible. The productive capacity of the land was decimated when water sources were closed up and terrace systems dismantled. Entire communities were destroyed. It seemed that the Romans were determined to remove the Jewish people from their homeland.

The enormous difficulties that were inflicted by the Romans resulted in large-scale emigration. Gradually, Israel lost its Jewish nature and culture as many fled, and Jewish leadership had to fight to preserve a national identity. Their most urgent desire was to restore religious life and to reassemble the Sanhedrin, the Jewish ruling council. All over Galilee, rabbis met in secret, and their decisions were spread clandestinely to the scattered Jews.

The widespread oppression lasted only until the death of Hadrian in 138; then slowly the Roman attitude towards the Jews and Judea began to relax. It was a heavy burden on Rome to maintain two legions – one fifteenth of the entire Roman army

– in such a small place. And the weakened nation, focused now on survival, no longer presented much threat of rebellion. The two strong wills that had collided frequently over two centuries came to a "Modus Vivendi," each accommodating the other in some ways, allowing a peaceable co-existence.

Antoninus Pius (138-161) replaced Hadrian as emperor. He was of Semitic descent, was familiar with the Jewish faith, and did not treat it as an enemy of Rome. In addition, some in the Roman Empire were beginning to question their own beliefs. The Greco-Roman gods had become less attractive and many people were drawn to religions that held a moral code, a promise of eternity, and spoke of a personal connection with God. Thus, the Jewish faith came to be regarded by many Romans as an admirable way of life.

At the end of the second century, the Roman-Jewish relationship had attained a decent level of mutual respect. Much credit for this is given to Rabbi Yehudah (Judah) HaNasi (the chief editor of the Mishnah, the Oral Law), and his Roman counterpart, the Emperor Septimius Severus (193-211). This convergence between Roman emperors and the Jews is also evidenced through inscriptions found in synagogues all over the Roman world: for instance, the house of Antoninus is mentioned as a friend of the Jews.

The following decades were a time of crisis in the Roman Empire; its enormous size required a large number of troops, and it was necessary to recruit non-Romans into the army in order to maintain a suitable military presence.

Signs of Decay in the Roman Empire

In 212 Roman citizenship was granted to everyone living in the empire. It was a controversial move, designed to increase the loyalty of the subject nations to Rome. The success was limited. Recruiting people from nations oppressed by Rome to serve Rome understandably caused a decline in the army's overall motivation and discipline.

The Roman army, now numbering some six hundred thousand, was kept busy defending the far-flung reaches of the empire. Along the Rhine River, the Danube, and from the Sassan (Persia), groups of barbarians and the armies of nearby nations pressed determinedly into Rome's territory.

> *"As the toes were partly iron and partly clay, so this kingdom will be partly strong and partly brittle. And just as you saw the iron mixed with baked clay, so the people will be a mixture and will not remain united, any more than iron mixes with clay." (Daniel 2:42-43)*

Through most of the third century, each Roman emperor's reign averaged two years. Chaos and instability began to insinuate themselves. The excellent Roman road system fell into neglect, and as a result, trade and commerce began to decline. The economic chaos, hard on the heels of the political uneasiness, also brought a rapid devaluation of the Roman coin. In Nero's day, silver and gold made up ninety-five percent of a coin's weight. By the end of the third century it was only five percent. In an effort to rebound, taxation was increased to a level that eventually led to the collapse of local economies throughout the empire.

As a border province of the Roman Empire, Israel was no doubt affected by the political and financial insecurity and the empire's increasing military vulnerability. In many cases, land that had been retained by Jews through the revolt, or later redeemed by them, was in the end sold to non-Jews. As much as the rabbis tried to prevent this, the farmers simply could not hold their land without the availability of skilled laborers and with the added burden of heavy taxes. Many discouraged farmers moved to the cities hoping to improve their lot; the cities grew rankly while the rural areas fell increasingly fallow.

The Ascension of Christianity

On a religious level, the power and influence of the Christian church began to increase. The number of Christians in Israel was constantly growing; fathers of the church such as Origin and Eusebius had settled in Caesarea, establishing a thriving religious center there. Although the Roman authorities continued to persecute Christians around the empire, in Israel more tolerance was shown. In many cases, Christians held influential positions in the imperial administration and even in the army. The Talmud informs us that numerous towns and villages exclusively inhabited by Christians could be found in Galilee and along the coast. In the case of Jews who had become followers of Yeshua – Jesus – they were still Jewish, and obviously still desired to live in their homeland. The enmity between Jew and Christian, fiery during the first century due to the Messianic claims of Jesus, had apparently ebbed enough that Messianic Jews were able to live peaceably in Israel. The sources covering this era do not reveal much about the degree of Jewish and Christian interaction. The pagan Roman Empire was still alive and it seems to have cast its historical shadow darkly over all else.

In the matter of a few decades, the Jews would not stand alone in their regard of the land of Israel as holy, and Christians, Jews, Samaritans, and pagans would be involved in bitter struggles over the land of Israel.

Christians in Israel remained a small minority. Nothing pointed to the tremendous change the Roman world would soon go through, especially the spread of Christianity and the influence that would accompany its new popularity. In Jewish centers around the Roman Empire, Judaism and Christianity had openly collided, but in Israel the interaction was at a lower level. There were no religious debates or any other kinds of dialog between the two – no sanctioned ones, at any rate. On the threshold of what came to be called the "Byzantine Era," when its influence would dramatically expand, the Christian faith had not yet significantly impacted Israel.

The Jewish leadership was busy keeping the social and religious structure of Israel intact – working to maintain the national leadership under rabbis in Israel, without ceding that power to their kinsmen in the large, wealthy Jewish enclaves in Babylon. (These were the descendants of those Jews who had remained there at the end of the Exile).

All over Europe, inside and outside the Roman sphere, Christianity was flourishing under adverse conditions. In a relatively short time, the new faith had won the hearts of many pagans, and the rift between Jew and Christian continued to expand.

While a purely humanistic perspective might view the widening breach between Jew and Christian as the result of a fierce competition for converts, it actually went much deeper than that. Christian and Jew had arrived at a point in history where their paths sharply diverged.

The Jewish perspective of Jesus was as a false Messiah. Unconverted Jews were still waiting for the Anointed One promised in Scripture; but in the mind and heart of the Christian, Jesus was th*e M*essiah, fulfilling every Old Testament Messianic prophecy.

The Christians believed that Israel was being punished – suffering the consequences – for its refusal to accept Jesus as the true Messiah. The devastated villages in Judea, the masses of people led in chains to exile, and the ruins on the Temple Mount seemed to support that claim.

Christ himself had said that Jerusalem's destruction came about because of their rejection of him:

> *"As he approached Jerusalem and saw the city, he wept over it and said, 'If you, even you, had only known on this day what would bring you peace--but now it is hidden from your eyes. The days will come upon you when your enemies will build an embankment against you and encircle you and hem you in on every side. They will dash you to the ground, you and the children within your walls. They will not leave one stone on another, because you did not recognize the time of God's coming to you.' " (Luke 19:41-44)*

The Jews, God's chosen people and the ancestors of Jesus, began to be regarded as enemies of Christ and no longer precious to God.

10

The Byzantine Era c. 312 - 637

Miles from Israel, outside the walls of Rome, a man named Constantine led his army to victory over the army of Maxentius and claimed the throne of the Roman Empire. The victory, on October 28, 312, marked the beginning of one of the largest revolutions in world history – the Christian revolution.

Initially, this change in government did not affect Israel, which was at the eastern side of the Roman Empire and therefore not under Constantine's dominion. The Emperor of the East (Lycinius) did favor the Christians, but this meant only that Christian persecution had ceased. No advantage was given to Christianity itself in Palestine, but the fact that now the Roman government was Christian caused great concern. The outcome, from a Jewish perspective, was the same: the hated Christian enemy enjoyed favor ahead of the Jews, and would soon become the greater authority in their own homeland.

While Rome had long tolerated religions other that its own – and the Jews were recognized as such – the new situation was different. Christian animosity toward Jews was growing, fueled by a growing perspective of the Jews as "Christ killers." Christianity by this time was several generations removed from the original influx of Jewish converts, and there was little brotherhood between the two groups. Christians worshipped the God of Israel, but their acceptance of Jesus as Messiah sliced a huge gulf between themselves and the Jews.

Constantine was fighting to win the whole empire; if he gained control of Lycinius' domain, persecution of the Jews was sure to increase.

On September 18, 324, the tug-of-war over the east ended when Constantine's army overpowered the army of Lycinius, and Israel became part of Constantine's empire. Christians assumed jurisdiction of the territory. Christian tutors were hired to educate the emperor's family and those of the Roman aristocrats.

This was also the year that Constantine announced his decision to move the empire's capital from Rome to "New Rome" – Byzantium – located in what is now Turkey. In 330 the city of Constantinople (modern-day Istanbul) became the capital of the empire. While there is some debate as to when the Roman Empire officially became the Byzantine Empire, we will date it from this event.

While Lycinius' few anti-Christian decrees were immediately lifted, the anti-Jewish rules of his pagan empire remained in force. Almost overnight, the Christians found themselves in a powerful position. Persecution of the Jews, including limiting their rights and removing their voice in government, began immediately.

As Christian influence grew, more decrees were enacted which discriminated against Jews: conversion to the Jewish faith was prohibited, and at the same time there was a dedicated effort to convert as many Jews as possible to Christianity.

As long as no other nation had any particular ties to the land, the dreams of the Jews – their longings for a consecrated Jerusalem and a restored nation – had seemed attainable. Now, with Constantine's personal interest in the land due to its Christian history, these hopes dimmed. All Christians now regarded Israel, once sacred to Jews alone, as holy to Christianity. They tried to eradicate the Jewish presence in Israel by destroying Jewish buildings and other evidences of Judaism.

The Jews saw Christians as appropriating what belonged to them – and watched helplessly as the imperial treasury funded the construction of Christian churches all over Israel, some standing defiantly on the very ruins of Jewish holy places. It seemed there was little chance that the two faiths could live peaceably in the same land.

The strong and continuing bond between the Jews in Israel and those still in Babylon also alarmed the Christian authorities. Babylonian Jews enjoyed religious freedom, and their open support was a great blessing to Israel's Jews during this difficult time.

In addition, the Jewish religious year – the exact dates of all religious observances – was now being calculated in Babylon rather than in Israel. When the Empire (seeking to cripple Jewish strength in Israel) passed laws to curtail open communication between the two, it was a severe blow.

The Galus Revolt

Political unrest and outside aggression are always potent invitations to those who live under the yoke of a foreign power, and both circumstances soon came into play in Israel: Constantine's death precipitated a civil war as his three sons disputed the throne. By 350, his oldest son, Constantius, had emerged as the victor. On March of 351, Constantius appointed his nephew Galus as "Caesar of the East." When this happened, Shabor, the king of Persia, led his forces deep into the Empire's territory.

For the Jews, the growing Christian presence was ominous – the rulers of the Byzantine Empire seemed bent on the eradication of Judaism. More than two hundred years had passed since the Jews had rebelled against the Roman Empire. They had chosen since that time to coexist peaceably, so that the nation might be saved from extermination; but the renewed strife ignited a still-smoldering spark: Jewish patriots, taking advantage of the unstable political situation and the advancing Persian army, rebelled against Byzantium.

As in the Bar-Kochba Revolt, there are only a few historical mentions of this uprising. It is impossible to tell whether it was fought using conventional armies, guerilla warfare, or only existed as small-scale, localized skirmishes. Christian sources are silent, which could mean that there were no formal Jewish-Christian military confrontations. Some sources suggest that the Jews attacked some of the pagan cities, and archeological digs have unearthed evidence that in Galilee and along the coast, several Jewish towns suffered some sort of disaster.

It is hard to imagine that an extensive revolt would be ignored by all but one Roman historian, thus we are led to conclude that the Galus Revolt was probably a minor uprising. This view is also supported by the fact that afterwards, the Jews maintained their privileges and no discriminating decrees were enacted as punishment.

The rebellion demonstrated anew that during precarious times, courageous and patriotic Jews were still willing to act. However, this revolt appears to have been the last time for centuries that the Jews, in any significant number, fought to reclaim their national existence.

The Emperor Julian

Although by now Christianity was considered a superior religion and the last two emperors had been Christians, paganism did not disappear without a fight. In fact, it was reintroduced from the highest level when Julian, the brother of Galus, became emperor of Rome in November 361.

As a student of Neo-Platonism (a mystical, polytheistic philosophy based on third century interpretations of Plato's writings) Julian believed in the existence of multiple gods. He hated the Christian religion – feeling that it had been forced upon him – and blamed it for the devaluation of Greek art, literature, and mythology, all of which he greatly admired.

Christian writers often refer to him as "Julian the Apostate" because he encouraged religious freedom and the rebuilding of pagan temples (many of which had been previously destroyed in the name of Christianity). He also rescinded many of the privileges his predecessors had granted to Christians.

The emperor blamed the Christians for the chaos in the empire and this had unexpected benefits for the Jews: as a non-Christian religion, they were free to attempt a restoration of the Temple and its sacrificial system, answering the hope of faithful Jews everywhere. The emperor approved an imperial decree calling on the Jews to do just that. With this official support, spirited riots broke out in Israel between Jews and Christians. It looked for a time as if the Jews would again gain the upper hand and that Christianity would decline.

Preparation began in Jerusalem for the rebuilding of the Temple, and the work commenced as the emperor Julian rode out of Antioch with his army to make war on Persia. In May of 363, fire broke out at the Temple construction site and the work was halted. The reason for the fire was unknown, although the Jews naturally believed Christians had set the blaze.

The actual cause of the fire became academic with the death of Julian in battle. A Christian emperor assumed his throne, the

Temple reconstruction was abandoned, and Christianity once again became the officially sanctioned religion of the empire.

However, the support that Julian's anti-Christian reforms had received from people throughout the empire was a warning to the Christian authorities that the empire as a whole was not committed to the Christian faith. In addition to the Jews, there were still powerful pagan groups with wide influence. Schisms were also beginning to develop among Christians, as certain doctrines came into dispute.

The Christian church had been attempting to codify Christian beliefs throughout the fourth century. The Council of Nicaea, which convened in 325, met for this purpose. A major point of concern was the portrayal of Jesus Christ: co-existent with God the Father, or created by Him? Out of this council came the Nicene Creed, which stated in part:

> *"One Lord Jesus Christ, the Son of God, begotten of the Father [the only-begotten; that is, of the essence of the Father, God of God], Light of Light, very God of very God, begotten, not made, being of one substance with the Father;"*

Some bishops attending the council refused to sign the creed. They held to a teaching by the theologian Arius, who lived in the area of Alexandria, Egypt, in the early fourth century. According to Arius, Jesus was divine, but he did not co-exist with God the Father eternally; instead, he was created by the Father and thus inferior to him. This teaching, while not widely held, contributed to the confusion and disagreement within the Christian world.

Israel's Growing Attraction to Christians

Upon Julian's death and the repeal of religious freedoms for non-Christians, governmental decrees took the form of anti-Jewish restrictions. The intent (to limit and isolate non-Christians in designated areas) was in fact welcomed by the Jewish leaders and gave the Jews opportunity to more easily preserve their own heritage and maintain their distinct culture. The tactic had success among the Hellenic pagans, however. In fact, by the middle of the sixth century, paganism was almost totally erased.

Jewish discrimination increased even more under the reign of the Emperor Theodosius and his son: Jewish religious life was restricted and it became illegal to convert non-Jewish slaves to Judaism; later it was declared illegal to even possess non-Jewish slaves.

The Jews were also prohibited from holding public office. However, it was in the empire's best interest not to restrict their financial activity and therefore Jews still enjoyed relative economical freedom and were able to travel and trade freely. Some new restrictions were imposed, but most of them were merely continuations of earlier ones.

All over the Byzantine Empire, the balance of power continued to favor the Christians, but in Israel, Jews possessed some autonomy: authorities still respected the Jewish judicial system and allowed their courts to remain functional. In fact, the reputation of Jewish justice caused many non-Jews to bring their appeals to Jewish courts rather than to the public ones.

Christian pilgrims began to make their way to Israel: the eastern part of the Byzantine Empire had become safer and Israel was gaining fame as a bountiful source of Christian relics. By offering up the bones of martyrs and boasting many churches of exceptional beauty, Israel became a destination site for those who were interested in the Christian world – even more so when Emperor Theodosius' wife, Eudocia, left Constantinople to live in Jerusalem. She launched several large-scale construction projects all over Israel.

As the Christian population grew, the tension between the opposing groups grew also. Synagogues were now the new preferred targets of those who desired to persecute the Jews. In many Jewish towns and in the mixed cities, Jewish facilities were attacked by mobs. Often the looters enjoyed at least the passive support of the authorities and were not punished.

The Office of Perfectos is Abolished

Suppression took public form as well. The head of the Jews, the position of Perfectos, was a title that conferred respect, influence, and financial wealth on the office holder. This was a hereditary position, denoting headship over all Jews.

Both pagan and Christian emperors had long sanctioned the position of Perfectos, since these men were very useful in maintaining law and order among the Jewish inhabitants in Palestine. However, a wealthy and respected Jew occupying a position of power within the Christian empire was unacceptable to some.

Despite an imperial decree that condemned any act against the Head of the Jews, the office of Perfectos was targeted by imperial prejudice. In 415 the Perfectos was accused of circumcising some of his pagan and Christian servants. He was also accused of building new synagogues. (The Jewish leadership considered these things within its rights and was unwilling to compromise on these issues.)

Many of the authorities in imperial leadership sought to eliminate the office, for the Perfectos by his very presence transformed the Jews from a melange of individuals into a cohesive nation.

In 429 the current Head of the Jews (Gamalio) died, leaving no son to replace him. The Byzantine authorities exploited the situation by abolishing the position of Perfectos and dividing the power among several Jewish leaders. This had the effect of splintering the Jewish community, as individuals rallied to their preferred leader.

For the Byzantines, abolishing the position did aid in subjugating the Jews, but it was a two-edged sword. Instead of dealing with one authority that represented all Jews, the Byzantine authorities were now forced to deal with several leaders, each with his own agenda.

Defining the Nature of Jesus

Christianity as a faith enjoyed power over Judaism, but it continued to experience its own internal divisions. At the Council of Nicaea, the debate had been about the relationship between the Father and the Son. The Council of Ephesus (in 431) dealt with another theological question – the person of Jesus – and sought to define the interaction between his divine and human natures. Some felt that he had two natures, as in half-man and half-god. Others believed that the Bible portrayed Jesus as having both natures completely.

At Ephesus, the elders reconfirmed the Nicene Creed and affirmed Jesus as one person, not two – as fully God and fully man. This did not settle the controversy, however, and Christendom wrestled to define its faith, meeting again in Chalcedon in 451.

The council at Chalcedon (part of the modern-day city of Istanbul) formulated the Chalcedonian Creed, declaring the "full humanity" and "full divinity" of Jesus. This decree effectively widened the gap that already existed in the church regarding the nature of Jesus, and would eventually lead to a formal division of the Christian church.

Now, in the eastern empire, as tension grew between the opposing Christian camps, the Jews were left more or less alone. As a religion, they no longer constituted a threat to Christianity. Furthermore, it was recognized that Jewish capital could be courted to finance future wars.

With each Christian faction treating the Jews as possible allies, the Jews in Israel enjoyed a period of relative serenity. Over roughly 85 years, from 438-527, not a single anti-Jewish decree came before the emperors of Byzantium, and there was unprecedented prosperity in Israel. Immigrants from Western Europe enriched the country's economy and visiting pilgrims left their coin behind. Despite their lower status, the Jews did not miss out on the new affluence. In archeological excavations, the beautiful mosaic floors discovered in ancient synagogues indicate that the Jews had definitely benefited from the wealth that flooded the land.

The Samaritan Revolts

There was another ethnic group in Israel – mostly silent for centuries – that carefully watched the course of events during this time: the Samaritans. As the Jews themselves had often been, the Samaritans were "between a rock and a hard place" under both Roman and Byzantine rule. Unrecognized by the Jews as Jewish, any privileges the Jews enjoyed were denied to the Samaritans.

Finally in 484 the first Samaritan revolt broke out. The short rebellion was brutally crushed by the Byzantine Emperor Zeno, and ended with the destruction of the Samaritan Temple on Mount Gerizim. A Christian church was built over the site.

Another attempted revolt began in 529. Trusting that Persia and perhaps the Jews would come to their aid, the Samaritans took over Caesarea and a few other key cities, establishing a kingdom. Their success was short-lived. The Byzantine army mercilessly crushed the revolt and sold thousands of Samaritans into slavery.

Rebellion against Byzantium, an empire motivated by religious zeal, was dangerous; that zeal promoted the annihilation of pagans. And unlike the Jews, the Samaritans had no community outside Israel to extend support or to offer a haven in exile. The Samaritans were totally defeated.

The Emperor Justinian (525-567)

When the emperor Justinian came to power, he decided to reinstitute many of the anti-Jewish decrees formulated during the reign of Theodosius, along with many new ones. For the first time, the Byzantine authorities began to involve themselves in strictly Jewish matters and the empire now dictated the form of worship in the synagogues.

Some synagogues were destroyed and churches erected in their places. Celebrating Passover was also forbidden, if in that specific year it fell prior to Easter. To ensure that the decrees were carried out, the Bishops were given special permission to report directly to Constantinople if the civil governor hesitated or was reluctant to execute the empire's policy. The first forced conversions to Christianity took place during this time.

Justinian's reign was the high point of the Byzantine Empire, but with his death the empire faltered. As happens so often in history, the loss of a powerful ruler without a strong successor is devastating to the kingdom that is left behind. Such was the destiny of the Byzantines in Israel.

After Justinian's death, the Persian army prepared to attack from the east. When Persia finally marched into Byzantine territory in 603, the Christian empire was already in chaos. The emperor Phocas was an illegitimate ruler and faced opposition from the empire's aristocracy.

The religious tensions inspired by the debate over the nature of Jesus had also heated up again. Most Christians living in Israel had rejected the beliefs codified by the Chalcedonian Creed – and they had suffered discrimination because of it. These Christians resisted the call to rally behind the Byzantine government, which officially supported the doctrine. In order to survive the Persian threat, unity was paramount; but the empire was disintegrating.

The Persian army marched on the Byzantine strongholds and conquered them one by one. Excitement percolated among the Jews as the Persians drew closer to Israel. Many soldiers in the Persian army were Jews and must have looked forward to the opportunity to liberate Israel.

While the Persian troops were on their approach, an open revolt began in Israel. The Jews and the few remaining Samaritans seized the opportunity to get even with the hated Christians. They openly welcomed the enemy. At the end of May in 614, the Persian army conquered Jerusalem and the ravaged city was handed over to the Jews.

Once again, historical sources do not reveal much: Jerusalem was in Jewish hands after the arrival of the Persians, but Jewish hopes for restoring the temple and the kingdom must have faded almost immediately. Despite the valuable help that the Jews had given, they were not granted enduring authority over Jerusalem or any part of Israel. The Persians wanted only to promote stability in the territory, and the Jews, at a mere 20 percent of the population, could not guarantee such stability. A few short months after the Persian army had liberated Israel, it was as if nothing had changed. Control over Jerusalem was handed back to the Christians.

While in Israel the events had turned against the Jews, on the battlefield the wheel turned against Persia. The Byzantine emperor Heraclius, in a bold attack, marched his troops to the rear of the Persian army, and threatened the Persian capital at Ktesiphon.

The Persians were forced to request a ceasefire. When Heraclius, victorious and having recovered the remains of the "true cross" from Persia, entered Jerusalem on March 21, 629, he came as a conqueror. He promised to give the Jews protection, but was pressured by Christian leaders and clergy to do otherwise. As far as they were concerned, the recent Jewish uprising required retaliation. The Jews were expelled from Jerusalem and the surrounding area. Many fled outside the country to Persian territory, and the small Jewish presence in Israel was once more almost completely erased.

The Byzantine Empire would continue to exist in different degrees for another 850 years, but as a force in Israel, it virtually disappeared. Byzantine emperors would continue to be interested in the affairs of Israel; to some extent they initiated the Crusades and were also involved financially in restoring

Christian holy sites. However, the days of Byzantine Israel were over.

Effects of the Byzantine Era on Israel

Israel was definitely impacted by the Byzantine presence. The population increased during this time, and areas that had been previously uncultivated were transformed into lush farmland. All over the country, archaeological evidence of Byzantine influence can still be found. The sizes of cities, churches and other ruins show that the Byzantine Era ushered in a high standard of living and Byzantine oversight resulted in an increase in the productive use of Israel's resources.

The Byzantine Era also birthed the Christian monastic movement, which was to have a lasting effect not only on Christianity, but on Israel as well. By the middle of the fourth century, Israel had several monasteries in the Judean desert. It was not unheard of for a single monastery to contain tens of thousands of these ascetics.

The monks isolated themselves willingly in their desert enclaves. Some were there because of a sincere desire to devote themselves completely to God; some from a misguided notion that for a Christian to be "not of the world" meant a physical withdrawal from it; still others were there for different reasons. Whatever the motives, the monastic movement flourished.

Monks spent their lives in solitude behind monastery walls all over Israel. They meditated, copied scrolls of the Bible, and remained isolated from the attractions of city life. The interaction between these hermits and others was minimal, but their way of life was nevertheless admired – monks were regarded as wise and pure examples of the Christian life and worthy of imitation.

During the time of the Crusades, the monastic ideal was to become uniquely entwined with the office of knight, eventually creating a type of military order that became invaluable to the Crusader effort.

11

The Early Muslim Era
c. 634 -1099

The Byzantines and the Persians (modern Iran) were spilling each other's blood, wrestling each other for control of Israel. At the same time, Bedouin mercenary tribes (who had been hired by Byzantium to guard the empire's eastern border) became increasingly unwilling to carry out their duties when their Christian masters failed to pay them regularly.

The Muslims, whose own territory was beginning to expand from the South (Arabia), were able to persuade the Bedouins to join their effort against the Byzantine Empire. In the first skirmishes the Muslims were driven away. Only after the death of Mohammed in 632 did Abu Bakr, the first Caliph (successor to Mohammed), launch a full-scale attack against the Byzantine Empire.

Religious zeal motivated the attack, but the new religion's "Jihad" or Holy War (spreading the faith by the sword), did not lack other attractions for the victors – the conquest of wealthy countries meant the acquisition of valuable resources. Additionally, Muslims who die in a Holy War are promised honors and riches usually unavailable to them in this life.

Since the Bedouin tribes were no longer protecting the Byzantine borders, the Muslim army easily reached the area of

Gaza. When the Byzantine army quickly mobilized, the Muslim commander sent for reinforcements. As the Muslim relief forces marched through the desert, they approached the enemy from the rear; the Byzantines were caught by surprise and were scattered.

This victory, on July 1, 634, signaled the collapse of the Byzantine Empire in Israel. All of the fortified cities except for Jerusalem and Caesarea fell quickly to the Muslims. Citizens who surrendered were speared; those who resisted were tortured. The fanatical Muslim army destroyed churches, monasteries, and other religious buildings in its holy zeal against the infidel.

Previously, the Byzantine Empire had dealt with foreign aggression in the east through bribery and negotiation. But the Muslims were immune to such approaches: their religious zeal did not allow for any kind of compromise as long as they were able to maintain a strong offensive.

One last attempt was made by the Byzantine Emperor Heraclius to save the eastern part of his empire: a massive army was concentrated in Syria at the end of 635 and into the following summer. The strength of this Byzantine force deterred the Muslim army, which began to retreat. However, careless planning led the pursuing Byzantine army into an ambush on the banks of the Yarmouk River; the Muslim forces were then able to defeat the larger Christian army. Jerusalem fell two years later, surrendering to escape destruction.

Some historians consider this one of the most significant battles in all of history, because it marked the first great Muslim advance outside of Arabia, and allowed the establishment of Islam in Christian Palestine, Syria and Mesopotamia – throughout the Middle East.

Muslim Taxation

At this time, even though damage had occurred during the Muslim invasion, the conquered settlers were still cultivating the farmland. Muslim law did not permit the recruited Bedouin tribesmen to dwell in the villages or to become farmers; like the Byzantines, the Muslims used the nomads only as mercenaries. The tribes were paid with the taxes that the Muslims levied on the defeated villagers.

This taxation was the main burden that the people in Israel bore. It was a somewhat normal burden for the Jews: living under religious and other restrictions for centuries had forced the Jews to adjust. They had long ago learned that taxation was the inevitable lot of the conquered.

For the Christians, though, it was a new situation; the restrictions they had inflicted upon the Jews were now being inflicted upon them. Christians were now also barred from public office. The Muslim masters showed their domination in some unique ways: they forced non-Muslims to dress differently that they might be easily distinguished from Muslims; and non-Muslims were forbidden to build houses that were larger than Muslim homes.

The economy was stable, remaining to a large extent in the hands of non-Muslims, since the Muslim government benefited economically from their knowledge and skills. The treasury was in constant need of the revenue provided by non-Muslims, since Muslims were not required to pay taxes.

This explains, at least in part, why there were no government-sanctioned attempts at forced conversion during the first centuries of Muslim occupation. Fewer converts meant higher tax revenues. Some Christians and Jews voluntarily converted to Islam in order to avoid taxes and take advantage of the inheritance laws, which favored Muslims.

The first years of the Muslim expansion were typified by an interesting problem – the Muslim territories were growing, but Muslim authorities lacked experience in administration and government. This issue was addressed by reinstating former Byzantine officials to the positions they had previously held.

Interaction between Muslims and non-Muslims continued to be limited; the different cultures lived side by side but had little in common. All in all, life under such conditions was relatively easy for both Jews and Christians.

Muslim Expansion

Within Islam, followers of Mohammed had been divided since his death over who should be his successor (Caliph). Those who believed Abu Bakr was the rightful successor came to be known as Sunni Muslims. Others, who believed he had wrested power for himself in violation of Mohammed's direct orders, are called Shiite Muslims. They believe that Ali Ibn Abu Talib, Mohammed's cousin and son-in-law, was the rightful successor.

Abu Bakr ruled for only two years until his death in 634. Three other Caliphs held power before the Shiite Ali Ibn Abu Talib finally assumed the Caliphate in 656, having fought several other challengers before securing the office. His assumption of power is considered to mark the major split between the Sunni and Shiite factions, which still exists today as a fierce and sometimes bloody rivalry.

Talib ruled for five years, until he was assassinated on January 24, 661. Muawiyah Ibn Sufian (Muawiyah I) took over as Caliph, and founded the Umayyad dynasty.

Islam continued on the offensive and Muslim troops invaded and conquered vast areas of Persia and North Africa and parts of Europe, such as Spain and Sicily. In most places the populations of the captured territories adopted the new religion, and the empire gained loyal allies to settle along its borders and fight for Islam.

The house of Umayyad based its headquarters in Damascus, thought to be the oldest continually inhabited city on earth. As the geographical center of the ever-growing Muslim territory, it occupied a strategic position. Damascus reached its zenith under the Umayyad dynasty, but the decision to make Damascus the capital had affronted those who regarded the holy cities of Mecca and Medina as the only possible centers of Islam. A revolt broke out against the Caliph. Israel, as always in the middle of things, was now caught in an Islamic civil war – the rulers of Hijaz (a region in the northwest of present-day Saudi Arabia, along the coast of the Red Sea), against the Caliph in Damascus.

Holy to Islam

One of the five main commandments of Islam concerns the Hajj. Every faithful Muslim is required to make a pilgrimage to one of Islam's holy places during his lifetime. However, the governor of the Hijaz, where the revolt was centered, had denied pilgrims access to the only Muslim holy places (Mecca and Medina), both located in his territory. Thus there was a need to provide an alternate site so that the pilgrimage requirement could be fulfilled. Jerusalem, while not mentioned in the Koran by name, and with no known connection to Mohammed, was proclaimed an Islamic holy place.

This was done by forging a connection between Jerusalem and the 17th chapter of the Koran, which records the journey of Mohammed from Mecca to the "most remote place." The Koran teaches that he ascended from there that night to receive the blessing of the heavenly host and Biblical figures also holy to Islam. The "most remote place" was identified as Jerusalem's Mount Moriah (the Temple Mount), and thus Jerusalem became an official Muslim holy place.

Around 692, Abed Al Maliq, the Caliph from the Umayyad dynasty, had a magnificent building erected on top of Mount Moriah – The Dome of the Rock. In 705, Ibn Al Walid (the son of Al Maliq) added another building – the Al-Aqsa Mosque. While the Dome of the Rock was a shrine, built in Christian style over the top of the mountain, the mosque was a house of worship.

Muslims did not immediately accept Jerusalem's elevated status. The reasons for now calling the city Al-Quds (The Holy) seemed dictated more by necessity than by revelation. It took centuries before mainstream Islam would treat Jerusalem as a true holy city. However, the magnificent buildings on top and around the Temple Mount enhanced the reputation of the city and drew many visitors.

Israel was beginning to recover from the destruction caused during the Muslim conquest – roads were repaired, walls were built, and new Muslim-style cities were added. Ramla, founded in 716, was declared the capital of the area newly named "Jund Filastin," one of the five districts in the Syrian section of the Arab-Muslim Empire.

As the Muslim population in Israel increased, the number of Jews and Christians declined. Most inhabitants in Israel were now people with nomadic roots, unaccustomed to either urban or rural life. The country that only a few decades before had been crowded and intensively cultivated began to change in appearance.

In part this was due to the tribes of nomads who still wandered the area's eastern borders. Since the days of Rome, they had been freely plundering scattered settlements along the eastern borders and commandeering the rich farmland for their livestock.

No previous conqueror had been able to control these tribes, and the Muslims had no better success. As the nomads' herds carpeted the landscape and consumed the vegetation, the once-productive soil became wasteland; farms failed, settlers left, and desolation claimed the land.

Abas' Rebellion

Islamic conquest had brought many nations under the wings of the new faith. Many of these nations – Persians, Turks and others – had converted in order to share in the benefits Islam guaranteed to every Muslim. However, converts could not be treated as equals to Arab Muslims, for that would affect the tax revenues due to the government.

Disappointed and frustrated by this prejudice, many non-Arab Muslims were unhappy with the Umayyad dynasty, and internal opposition was growing. While the Caliph was occupied with Byzantine efforts to overthrow him, the discontent flared into open revolt. Led by Abas, a distant relative of Mohammed's family, Muslim rebels conquered Damascus in 750. The last Caliph of the house of Umayyad, having fled to Egypt, was caught and killed.

Until Abas' victory, Islamic power had been completely in the hands of Arabs, a people from a provincial desert culture. The best privileges of the faith were withheld from non-Arabs. The house of Abas, supported mostly by the Persian Muslims, came from a much different background: more sophisticated, more liberal, and willing to learn from other cultures and societies. The new regime moved the capital to a newly founded city on the banks of the Tigris River: Baghdad. The change in geography meant an ethnic change as well. The Arabs lost their important positions as those positions began to be filled by Turks and Persians.

In 868, Ahmed Ibn Tulun, the Shiite governor of Egypt, rebelled against Baghdad and proclaimed himself a Caliph. Suddenly all over the Muslim world, other local rulers proclaimed their independence and declared war against Baghdad. The Abbasid (Sunni) Empire of Baghdad was not able to effectively protect its vast area against so many challengers, and Islam splintered as struggles began to focus on internal divisions – especially that between the Sunnis and the Shiites. The Fatimids, a Shiite dynasty, conquered Egypt in 969 and a year later conquered Israel, which would remain in Shiite hands until the time of the Crusades.

The Fatimids

With ambitions to conquer Baghdad and become the supreme rulers of Islam, the Fatimids needed a large army and adequate financing for the task. With a new Muslim fleet based along the Mediterranean Sea, exploiting the trade that came through, the Fatimids brought much prosperity to Israel. Jews were also involved in the Fatimid government in Egypt. Descendants of Jews who had lived in Egypt since the dissolution of the Northern Kingdom (Israel), their influence proved beneficial to the Jews now living in their ancestral homeland.

Because of its geographic position, Israel once more became a host battlefield: the Fatimids (based in Egypt) and the house of Abas (based in Mesopotamia) engaged in a long war on Israel's soil.

Matters were getting worse in Israel for non-Muslims. The reign of the Fatimid Al-Hakim brought religious oppression, and both Jewish and Christian holy places in Jerusalem were defiled and destroyed. The Church of the Holy Sepulcher was demolished. The Muslim authorities were more tolerant of the Jews than of the Christians: the Christian connection to the hated Byzantine Empire made them the objects of intense Muslim persecution.

Changes in Society

The Muslim conquest had preserved the Byzantine infrastructure, and so for the first several decades the economy was not damaged and non-Muslims were reasonably treated. However, since Muslim society was primarily tribal, the tensions among the different clans surfaced soon after the glory days of the conquest had passed. When Muslims of non-Arab descent began to deprive Arab Muslims of lucrative posts, open war ensued. Added to the socio-economic issues was continual religious hostility.

The Sunnis and the Shiites had been at odds since the death of Mohammed and the naming of his successor. Now, the many nations that had been added to the Muslim world began to factor in the religious conflict. The Eastern nations of Persian descent hated the (Sunni) Arabs and thus sided with the Shiites. The Turks, in the northeastern extremity of the Muslim world, aligned themselves with the Sunnis. The tensions within the Muslim world were unrelenting.

Nearly a thousand years earlier, the conquering Greeks had introduced a new way of life into the region. They had hoped to integrate all the nations in the world into their culture, embracing all peoples and all faiths. The Muslims had no such desire. In considering Islam the superior religion and culture, they were strongly determined to live separated and isolated within Israel.

The Arabs, the founders of Islam and its main ethnic body, eventually lost their majority in it: the newcomers soon took over Islam and changed it for good. By the end of the eleventh century, Israel was a country full of diverse eastern peoples (most of whom were Muslim) and many Arabic-speaking Christians, Jews, and Samaritans. The wars, ethnic mistrust, and perpetual animosity between Arabs and non-Arabs, Sunnis and Shiites, had divided the Muslim world into an endless number of Emirates, Sultanates and Caliphates, each with its own interests. When Europe later sent its warriors into the land of Islam, these divisions made the Crusaders' initial victories relatively easy.

Since the Muslim world was increasingly divided and turbulent, the Byzantine armies continued to invade. After four centuries of conflict, the well-managed farmlands and efficient administration once established by the Byzantines no longer existed. Both the land and its people were exhausted.

The Byzantines took advantage of this and frequently attacked from the sea, crippling the Muslim harbors along the Israeli coastline. Eventually, the Byzantine army was able to march victoriously to Antioch, hoping to move further inland and liberate Jerusalem. They turned to the Western church for help.

12

Introduction to the Crusades c. 1095 – 1100

Even today, the circumstances that produced the Crusades are not well understood. The historical events are of course a matter of record; however, the electrified atmosphere that so unified the people is still hard to explain. At this time in Europe there was a stark definition between the classes – noblemen, clergy, and peasants. Seemingly, there were no common interests to bring together all Christians to stand for the same cause, at least no earthly ones.

The trigger that shot hundreds of thousands of Christians into the Levant was pulled on November 27, 1095, in a conference held by Pope Urban II in Clermont, France. His plea is considered today to be one of the most effective speeches in history.

Earlier that year, at the Council of Piacenza, Pope Urban had received an appeal from the Byzantine Emperor requesting military assistance against the Seljuk Turks. Later, at the conference at Clermont (a small gathering attended by about 300 clerics), the Pope urged the knights in France and England to undertake a military pilgrimage to Israel.

He declared a "bellum sacrum" (Christianity's own Holy War), and called on the knights to liberate the Holy Sepulcher, the location marked as the grave from which Jesus had risen.

What made the time right for such a step? Was the Pope's main concern for Jerusalem – or were there other compelling reasons for this call to arms? One cannot rule out genuine alarm regarding the Christian holy places in Palestine. After the deliberate destruction of the Church of the Holy Sepulcher by the Egyptian Caliph Al Hakim in 1009, the Emperor of Byzantium had it rebuilt in 1030. But the church could do little to assure the safety of such places without the consent and cooperation of the Muslim authorities – which were by no means guaranteed. The recovery and protection of Christian holy sites was certainly a factor in Urban's charge to the knights, and the enthusiasm with which it was received.

However, other considerations were also at play. In 1054, after centuries of debate and disagreement, the eastern Christian world – under Byzantine rule – had refused to any longer acknowledge the Pope as its spiritual leader, and broke from the western church. This had left the Pope without influence or power over a significant part of the Christian world.

Thus, when the Byzantine Emperor asked Urban II for assistance against the Seljuk Turks, Urban may have seen the request as an opportunity not only to recapture the Holy Land for Christianity, but in so doing, to restore Papal authority over the eastern church.

It is possible that Urban was echoing an idea that had already been detailed in a letter sent by Pope Gregory VII to the German Emperor Henry 4th in 1074. In this letter, Pope Gregory put forth a plan to gather a large army from among the western kingdoms and to lead it to the aid of Byzantium – also with the aim of accomplishing the reunification of Christendom. Twenty years later, Urban's call to liberate Jerusalem – not Constantinople – put forth the same plan, but with a different incentive, one much more likely to stir the hearts and minds of those who heard it.

Hundreds of messengers were sent all over Europe to raise funds and recruit an army. The response was amazing. The mention of Jerusalem caught everyone's imagination, and as the cry went out to liberate Jesus' tomb – the place were he had risen – men of all classes and occupations responded. What forces of the heart drew these men? As with the Pope, spiritual fervor toward a holy cause was surely a great motivator, and perhaps, for many, the highest call.

But there are also other reasons men willingly go to war: European knights and the aristocracy probably recognized an opportunity to gain new wealth and property. In addition, the often-savage wartime behavior of the knights was sanctioned by the church under such circumstances, and thus offered the knights the ability to elevate their reputations and gain honor on the battlefield.

The peasant saw a unique chance to improve his way of life and free himself from the miserable conditions in which he lived. A spontaneous migration began all over Europe as groups of peasants headed to Palestine, entirely on their own.

Four large armies were assembled in Western Europe. Knights from France, Germany, England and Flanders, also accompanied by a battalion of knights from Sicily, prepared for the long journey to the Holy Land. With only princes of lower stature included in the ranks, it was decided that the Papal delegate should be the commander of the combined armies.

The First Crusade

Thus began a three-year odyssey. In July 1097, after crossing the straits of the Bosporus, the Crusader Army stood face to face with the Seljuks, the Turkish forces who had stymied the Byzantines. The two armies engaged in battle, and the Crusader victory opened the way into central Asia Minor and Palestine.

However, the lack of true military leadership and the desire of individual knights and princes to promote their own interests almost led to disaster. Instead of uniting in an effort to achieve the stated goal of the Crusade (the liberation of Jerusalem), some of the army turned to the east to assist the Armenians; others wanted to stop and conquer Antioch and other cities on the way to Jerusalem.

With the original goal of the journey seemingly forgotten, the commoners who had joined the Crusade presented an ultimatum: they would withdraw from the camp unless the armies proceeded immediately to Jerusalem. The threat had the desired impact: the knights and princes reconsidered their strategy and led the march to Jerusalem. By mid-June of 1099, the Crusaders encircled the walls of the city and placed it under siege.

Three weeks later, on July 15, 1099, the siege came to a successful end when the walls were breached and the inhabitants massacred. With more than twenty thousand dead bodies covering the streets of Jerusalem, the conquering army offered up thanks to God in the Church of the Holy Sepulcher.

Though Jerusalem stood under the Crusader flag, the task of conquering the whole country had just begun. Many of the knights scattered throughout Palestine, intent on claiming large estates for themselves. However, most of the participants in the First Crusade had never intended to make Palestine their new home; they headed back to Europe.

On this First Crusade, several fiefdoms had been established – the kingdom of Edessa (in northern Mesopotamia), and the earldoms of Tripoli and Antioch. By creating these countries along the shores of the Mediterranean, the Crusaders were able to hinder Muslim access to the sea – an important factor in protecting the new kingdom.

The Crusader strategy was three-fold: to build fortifications along the borders, to somehow prevent the unification of Muslim forces in the area, and to encourage European immigration in order to tip the ethnic scale in their favor.

Once in possession of Jerusalem, the Crusade leaders had to decide on its government. The clergy wanted to declare the Holy Land a papal state and invite the Pope to rule. The secular aristocracy called for a European monarchy. The peasants, seeking new freedoms and greater economic opportunity, didn't want to live under a government that simply reproduced the same form of life they had fled in Europe.

It was impossible to crown a king, for there was no one qualified for the title. Eventually, Godfrey of Bullion, one of the leaders of the First Crusade, was named the ruler of the New Latin Kingdom. He was given the title "The Protector of the Holy Sepulcher" and placed at the head of the new government.

The Feudal System of Europe Displayed in Israel

As the feudal system was practiced in Europe, society was divided into classes. There was little social interaction among the different groups. Each knew its place, its rights, and its duties. Transition from one class to the other was almost impossible. The Latin Kingdom of Jerusalem was modeled after a European kingdom. Therefore, the new government naturally embraced and implemented the feudal system in dealing with its subjects and determining social policies.

Knights were the backbone of the new kingdom and the main source of skilled manpower. Several hundreds of them dwelt in the urban Christian centers, with only few in the rural areas.

The Barons and Magnates were the knight-lords of larger estates. Under the feudal system, they were given an income, sometime in cash, sometimes a taxed portion of the income of a village. In return, they were at the king's beck and call. These landlords each had several knights serving under them. Each knight was directly linked to his master, who gave him his "Feudum," or means of existence, which the knight earned through various acts of protection or aggression.

The European practice of retaining a knight's loyalty through gifts of land or currency presented a major challenge in this diminutive new country, which was mostly populated by potential enemies – Muslim farmers. The amount of land in Crusader hands was relatively small.

Since land was limited, applying the feudal system in the Latin Kingdom resulted in a limited number of knights, which affected the military strength of the kingdom. Less than three decades after the kingdom was established, newly arrived knights found that though needed for protection, they were not always welcome to stay.

The Knights

Knights were a class unto themselves. Some came with the First Crusade as poor men from poor families, hoping that a powerful man, perhaps even the king himself, would notice their bravery and reward them. Others came from wealthy, influential families with guaranteed status in the king's court, and did not need to distinguish themselves for favors. Some of the minor knights, those who came with the First or Second Crusades, did very well in the new country – establishing dynasties that would figure in European politics in years to come.

Nonetheless, the knights, while skilled in warfare and important for that reason, were not an economically productive class. Trade and commerce, the lifeblood of any economy, were in the hands of the commoners – merchants and farmers. The knights earned their keep by protecting the merchants and the farmers, and in return were paid by the king. These mutually beneficial relationships were the pillars stabilizing the Crusader kingdom.

The Communes

The Latin Kingdom also produced a unique social class that represented both blessing and threat: the communes. The leaders of the First Crusade, desperately in need of an advantage by sea, had negotiated with the marine powers of Italy, France and Spain: in return for besieging Egyptian coastal cities with their superior navies, these countries received from the Latin Kingdom economic privileges and land, on which they built their own isolated communities.

Venice, Genoa and other European naval powers fully exploited the Crusaders' need in this area. In fact, one third of the kingdom's territory was owned by foreigners who lived in the communes: men who did not take orders from the king, who did not serve in the army, and who looked exclusively after their own interests – entirely free from the duties required of the common people.

The Balance of Power in the Latin Kingdom

In the first decades of the Latin Kingdom's existence, the rulers preserved the power of the monarchy. The first several were very careful about giving away land or other assets. The royal estates were larger than all of the knights' estates combined.

Among the many groups that comprised the Crusader kingdom's society (and also demanded a share of the land) was the Latin Church. Because the impetus for the Crusades had been essentially religious, the secular leaders of the country were compelled to recognize the Latin Church's authority. When a new king was installed, the Latin Patriarch of Jerusalem would place the crown of royalty on his head as a symbolic act that the king's power came from God; therefore he must submit to God and to His earthly representative (the Pope or someone with papal authority).

However, in reality the Latin Church was much weaker in the east than it was in Europe. The "Feudas" (land property) that had been given to the church to support its clergy was limited, and the holdings were small and scattered.

The Balance of Faith in the Latin Kingdom

Before the Muslim assault of Palestine, hundreds of Christian churches had been established across the country. But after four centuries of Muslim rule, the Christian population had been severely reduced. Some had fled the country, and many others had forsaken the Christian faith in order to enjoy benefits granted only to Muslims.

Over the centuries, at various ecumenical councils, the Roman Church had continued to codify certain beliefs. Each time, the churches disagreeing with the theological conclusions of the councils had split from the Roman church. Many of these churches (now called by such names as Oriental, Eastern, and Assyrian or Nestorian Orthodox) were based in the Middle East. Virtually all of the Christians in the Holy Land were of the Eastern tradition, whose theologies differed considerably from the Latin (or Roman) Church.

The manuscript of Pope Urban's speech in Clermont has been lost. Different versions abound, but the main message in each of them is the urgent need to rescue the "Eastern brothers" in the Holy Land – the guardians of the Christian holy sites. With the exception of the Byzantine church (which agreed with the Roman church in theological matters but refused to accept the authority of the Pope), the eastern churches were in effect excommunicated from the Roman Church and considered apostate. Now, the leaders of the Latin Kingdom faced a theological problem: in what way should they interact with these churches, which were the "Eastern brothers" they had come to rescue? And the Eastern churches faced their own dilemma: how should they regard the authority of the Roman Church?

The Greek Orthodox patriarch made his decision by fleeing from Jerusalem when the army of knights was on its way. The Crusaders, upon their arrival and conquest of the city, immediately appointed a Latin patriarch.

All over the country, Latin clergy were installed in high positions in place of the local clergy, who had generally been appointed by the Byzantine Emperor. In response, the Byzantines simply reappointed their own choices to the same offices, ignoring Latin authority.

Another debate that surfaced soon after the conquest involved the future of the holy sites. Although the Pope's call had been to rescue the Church of the Holy Sepulcher, it was in fact already under Christian control through the Eastern Church.

The Latin Church, claiming authority through the Crusader victory, took control of the holy sites away from the Eastern believers. Eventually, many of the Eastern believers felt their "Western brothers" were so unwelcoming that they left the country.

Military Orders in the Latin Kingdom

Although in almost every aspect the Latin Kingdom was an imitation of a contemporary European kingdom, one particular system was developed in the Latin Kingdom that paralleled nothing already in place in Medieval Europe: the religious military orders. These were organized military groups whose ideal member was a unique combination of knight and monk.

In Europe, The first orders of monks had been founded with the idea of practicing life as it was imagined to be in Jesus' day. Monks were the idealization of willing poverty, celibacy and the spiritual life.

As for knights, the romanticized idea that we have today about knighthood is based to a large extent on motion pictures that have portrayed the knight as hero, the "good guy" in the story. That was hardly the case in the eleventh through the thirteenth centuries. Many knights, on their deathbeds, had to repent of the lives they had led, lives full of avarice and bloodshed.

It was impossible to discipline the knights. The lords of the bigger estates – those who whispered in the king's ear and were part of the administration – were less tempted to disobedience. But the common knight had to prove himself. He did this by traveling around the continent, seeking the right opportunity.

In many ways the knights were no more than professional troublemakers.

The development of tournaments during feudal times was an attempt to allow the knights to exercise their savage natures in a setting overseen and controlled by the authorities.

Therefore many knights were attracted to the Crusades as a sanctified outlet for their warlike passions and a justification for their way of life. They found in the Crusades the opportunity to channel the aggression they could not display in society into the honorable profession of a Christian soldier fighting for Jesus.

Creating a religious military order where the aspects of monk and knight would be combined in one office was ingenious: monks were revered for their service to the community and were God's humble servants. Knights, while worldly, were still seen as strong and courageous warriors. These new military orders became the scaffolding that supported the Latin Kingdom. Significantly, they operated under the sole authority of the church, which continually sought more power in the new kingdom.

The first order, the Hospitalers (later known as The Knights of St. John), had been organized even before the Crusades, as a group that offered medical treatment and accommodations to Christian pilgrims visiting Jerusalem. The Knights Templar, founded in 1118, was the first order with the stated goal of training warrior monks. The Theothonians, the order of German knights, was founded outside the walls of Acre during the siege of the city in 1191. (The Germans adopted Templar principles but formed a strictly national order.)

Members of the various orders were employed as armed escorts for the caravans of pilgrims traveling in the Holy Land. The roads were not safe, as the government had ceased policing them due to the limited number of people available to patrol them.

Muslim forces continued to frequently raid Christian territory, sometimes with the permission of the local Christian lord. Pilgrims, and the money they spent during their visits, were significant contributors to the kingdom's treasury. Therefore, it was vital that the pilgrims be well protected.

These military orders benefiting the kingdom on many levels, and since they were well trained and quick to respond, the orders were eventually given more and more responsibility. At the peak of their power, the military orders could call to service the same number of knights as were controlled by the king. No doubt the crown was always reluctant to transfer additional authority to the church, but there was little choice.

The soldiers of the military orders were not ordinary knights. They were knights who were totally dedicated to serving Christendom, as guardians of the holy places and the whole Christian world. It was only natural that the task of preserving the Crusader kingdom's security should fall to them.

The fact that the new orders doubled the military capacity of the kingdom was a great blessing, but each of these military orders was in essence a tool of the Vatican. Instructions for the warrior monks came directly from the Pope's chambers, and sometimes the goals of the Church differed sharply from the needs of the kingdom.

Large estates all over Europe were given to the knights of these orders. This eased the economic pressure of the Latin Kingdom (which would otherwise be responsible for their sustenance) but it also assured that the loyalty of the knights would tend toward Europe rather than their country of service. In a relatively short time, the various military orders became some of the biggest landlords in Europe. The records show that the Knights of St. John's owned over nineteen thousand estates in Western Europe.

The need for fortresses grew as Muslim attacks against the kingdom intensified. The ownership of all royal fortresses was soon transferred to the new military orders. Over the second half of the twelfth century, more than half of the fortresses in Palestine were in their hands. The government gave multiple concessions to the military orders: their taxes were waived, and they could build their own churches, even if local ones already existed. This was a lucrative venture if they could lure people (and thus their economic support) away from the established church.

The power and autonomy of the military orders was also demonstrated by the fact that the Latin Kingdom's judicial system was given no authority over them. If a member of a military order committed an offense in the eyes of the kingdom, the kingdom was forbidden from exacting punishment (although the order could choose to chastise the offender). No doubt the court's authority, and that of the king, was frequently undermined.

In short, the military and the economy of the Latin Kingdom were essentially in the hands of people who were not first and foremost "kingdom minded." The communes were interested only in lucrative trade, and the military orders were committed to the kingdom's safety only when it suited their own purposes.

Although the army of the First Crusade had inscribed its banner with many noble sentiments, when the time came to implement them, the founders of the Latin Kingdom found little reason to change what they were used to from home. The Crusade leaders never could create – or maybe was not interested in creating – the kind of society that many had hoped for.

Methods of Warfare in the Latin Kingdom

In the west, chivalry and the idealism of knighthood had long dictated a mindset that resulted in a certain mode of warfare. Armies had met all over Europe using the same kinds of weapons, the same siege works, and the same military formations, little changed in centuries. Wars would usually focus on the skills of the knights. When European armies engaged the enemy, the infantry (the peasants – hardly trained, let alone equipped) would fight at the front of the formation, and the mounted knights followed up at the rear, ready to charge the enemy when a path was cleared.

Sometimes, so impatient were the knights that the order to charge was given while the infantry was still fighting hand-to-hand with the enemy. When this happened, the knights, astride magnificent horses, would ride to meet the foe – through and usually on top of their own infantry. Sometimes this caused more casualties than their opponents could claim.

The Crusader army was trained to charge in a ranked line, the infantry marching behind their shields and the knights riding shoulder to shoulder – all trusting that the impact of their heavy armor would mow down the enemy. This tight formation had always been the key to success in European conflicts. When they began to meet the Muslims on the battlefield, however, the Crusaders found that they faced a foe whose tactics and strategies were like nothing they had encountered before.

The biggest challenge facing the Crusader forces was the mounted archer. The European knight considered that an archer was spineless and faint-hearted because he chose to engage at a distance rather than meet his enemy face to face. However, even as the knights decried such cowardice, the Muslim archers were claiming many Crusader victims, drawing only close enough to launch their arrows before retreating a safe distance away. If it was cowardly warfare, it was also extremely efficient.

The Crusaders were forced to adjust their own tactics, and began to use mounted archers in their own armies. Since it was still considered inappropriate for a European knight to fight as an archer, these bowmen were recruited from the local Eastern Christians. Had the European knights "lowered themselves" to perform as archers, the entire social structure of Medieval Europe might have been challenged.

Holy Land Fortifications and other Construction

Since the Crusaders were never able to create a Christian majority in the kingdom, the only way to defend the land was by building fortresses along the highways and fortifying the cities. Building with stone was a challenge to the Crusader engineers, who were accustomed to working with timber and soil, but they elevated the art of stone construction to a level that up until then was unknown in Europe.

Many fortresses were erected along the borders, facing the two traditional enemies of the Latin Kingdom: Egypt and Syria. The fortress, including a dungeon, would be surrounded by a dry moat and one or two sets of walls. Some fortresses could accommodate hundreds of knights. Supplied with food and water, those within it could withstand a long siege.

When the army was mobilized, the troops were concentrated in the fortresses to prepare for war. During times when the army needed to withdraw from the battlefield, the fortresses served as sanctuaries providing a place to recover and regroup. They were also strategically located in order to provide intelligence about approaching enemy forces. In many cases, the stronghold would become the nucleus of a new village or town.

The religious architecture of this period was also sophisticated. Israel had never seen such an upsurge of construction: in addition to the existing Eastern churches, every commune, military order, and Crusader settlement had its own church.

Most of them were simply designed as massive buildings, often having more the look of a fortress than of a church. The Crusader architecture can be categorized as Romanesque – combining Roman and Byzantine elements of the ninth through the twelfth centuries, with rounded arches and barrel vaults.

The interiors of the churches (some of which were buildings erected before the Crusader era by the Byzantines or the Muslims) were decorated with mosaics and paintings. While numerous and large in scope, perhaps only a few of these Crusader edifices can be called "magnificent." One of them is the Church of the Holy Sepulcher, which, according to many sources, was one of the main building projects of the twelfth century.

Later, after the Crusaders had finally been expelled from the land, many of these churches and other monuments were demolished. Most of those that were spared became Muslim schools and mosques. What ruins that are still identifiable stand as stoic witnesses to Medieval Christendom in Israel.

13

The First Latin Kingdom c. 1100 - 1188

Following the death of Godfrey (the first ruler of the Latin Kingdom), his brother Baldwin 1st was named as his successor. Baldwin was the first of the Latin Kingdom's rulers to assume the title of King. His greatest challenge was to maintain order while the young country remained under constant pressure from the Muslims, who surged in repeatedly. In some cases, the townspeople simply waited behind the walls of their cities for the Muslim army to disperse.

In 1113 the Muslims surrounded the Crusader army for 26 days, and chaos erupted all over the kingdom: farmers refused to farm the fields; Muslims turned on Christian neighbors. However, the Muslims neglected to press their advantage, and the armies were stalemated: eventually the Muslims withdrew and an uneasy peace settled back over the land.

Baldwin later made a bold attempt to enlarge his kingdom's territory: he sent his army across the Jordan River in 1115 and gained control of the main caravan route connecting Egypt and Syria. This Christian wedge on the eastern side of the Jordan meant that commerce between the two main Muslim centers would require the payment of tribute to the hated Christians.

The Christian presence also meant that for several decades, the Latin Kingdom controlled the Muslim pilgrims' route to Mecca. This was a painful thorn in the side of the Muslim world. Baldwin's knights also invaded further south into the Negev Desert, as far as the Red Sea and Eilat. These raids were designed to destroy Muslim morale and gain a strategic advantage over the targeted Muslim principalities.

The most courageous of all of Baldwin's plans was his assault on Egypt. In eleven days (March 10-21, 1118), with two hundred and sixteen knights and four hundred foot soldiers, Baldwin crossed the Sinai Peninsula and invaded Egyptian soil. Baldwin knew that conquering Egypt with such a small force was impossible, but the bold move increased the Egyptians' sense of insecurity and thus justified the journey. On the way home, King Baldwin 1st died, having fallen ill in Egypt.

The reign of Baldwin 2nd (a relative of the previous king) in many ways mirrored the reign of his predecessor: dedicated to expanding his territory, he was constantly involved in various conflicts. He was taken as a prisoner of war in 1123-1124 while patrolling the kingdom of Edessa, but was released after a short time in captivity.

The Turks, Seljuks, and Arabs were still fighting each other. Even though each group could call on an incredible number of troops, the Crusader kingdom held the edge militarily as long as the Muslims stayed at each other's throats.

To the north, however, the inter-tribal animosities were beginning to be set aside: Zangi, the King of Mosul (in Iraq), had been able to unite various Arab forces under his leadership. This new cooperation had a specific effect on the northern Crusader kingdoms of Antioch and Edessa, which had become the victims of numerous assaults and were slowly losing ground.

Since the Emirate of Damascus had provided a physical buffer zone between Arab interests and the Latin Kingdom for many years, the Latin king at this time (Foulk of Anjou, the son-in-law of Baldwin 2nd) was unaware of or underestimated the threat Zangi represented, and remained unaware until it was too late.

When Zangi's forces laid siege to Damascus in 1139, King Foulk sent troops to rescue his ally. Zangi then turned all his efforts toward the smaller and weaker Latin principalities: Antioch, Tripoli and Edessa. The latter was the easiest target; its position between the Tigris and the Euphrates was particularly vulnerable, and only a few Latin Crusaders made up the local aristocracy. The rest of the inhabitants were Muslims and Armenians.

Over several years, repeated attacks on Edessa's main fortresses weakened both its military strength and its economy. By this time (1144) King Foulk had died. The new ruler was his 14-year-old daughter, Melisande. She dispatched her army, but it was too late. Had the prince of near-by Tripoli also sent his troops, Edessa might have been saved.

Instead, on December 29 1144 the walls of Edessa were breached and the Muslim army stormed the city, butchering its Christian inhabitants. The first Christian kingdom planted in the Levant was rudely cut down.

The Second Crusade

Soon afterwards, delegations from all over the Christian world stormed Rome to ask Pope Eugenius III to call for another Crusade to retake Edessa. On December 1st 1145, a Papal bulla, encouraging Christendom to engage in another Crusade, was published. Once again, Europe embarked on a religious quest.

Bernard de Clarivaux, the most influential theologian of the 12th century, was the man responsible for the electrified atmosphere. He appeared before King Louis 7th of France on March 31, 1146, and his impassioned words prompted King Louis to recruit an army of knights and requisition provisions for the journey.

Bernard called on everyone in the Christian world who wanted to purify his soul – regardless of his military skills or sect in society – to join the Crusade. His efforts bore fruit in Germany also when the Emperor Conrad agreed to "take the cross."

Tens of thousands of soldiers, peasants, and even criminals streamed out from Germany and France. The Germans set off in April of 1147 and soon afterwards, King Louis gave his own armies the order to leave for the Orient.

It is hard to tell what, if any, lessons the leaders of the Second Crusade learned from the mistakes made half a century earlier. No doubt prior knowledge of the topography and the hazards of the journey through Asia Minor would have benefited this Second Crusade, led by the mighty powers of Europe.

But the fact of the matter is that the Second Crusade was a bitter failure. Most of the German army was devastated in Asia Minor by mounted Seljuk archers and other local Muslim rulers who had finally united against the Christian enemy. The French army suffered heavy losses navigating their way over the same path the armies of the First Crusade had taken.

By the time the remnants of the German and French forces reached the Latin Kingdom and Antioch in early 1148, it was too late: they had lost their momentum and were unable to make a difference.

Nevertheless, the kings of Europe didn't want to leave the area without some achievement that would help to justify Europe's enormous investment in the venture. The Crusaders attempted to conquer Damascus, and were turned away in defeat. Beaten and frustrated, Conrad of Germany left the area in September 1148 and half a year later, Louis of France followed.

Europe had put its best resources together and accomplished nothing. Someone had to be blamed for the catastrophe. The Western Europeans blamed the Emperor of the Byzantines. Theologians and religious leaders portrayed the failure as God's punishment for the impurity and immorality in the Crusaders' camps.

The impotence the Second Crusade also marked a turning point in the balance of power between Christian and Muslim in the Levant. It had been demonstrated that the Christian world was as divided as the Muslim: The Byzantines, the Western Europeans, and each Crusader kingdom had its own agenda, and no longer even pretended the solidarity of the past.

Decades would pass before the memories of the Second Crusade had faded, the participants were all dead, and all the reasons for the failure forgotten. Only then would Europe try again.

Still After Egypt

In Jerusalem, the situation continued to deteriorate. Melisande remained as regent until 1152, when her son, Baldwin 3rd' turned 21 and was to be crowned as king. Melisande, backed by a powerful coalition of clergy and aristocracy, refused to cede her power. When her son was finally crowned on Easter Sunday of 1152, the kingdom teetered on the brink of civil war.

When the kingdom was partitioned between the two a short peace resulted, but in a few months Baldwin marched on Jerusalem (which was in his mother's hands) and conquered it.

Melisande was forced to accept a truce, keeping in her hands only the small principality of Nablus (north of Jerusalem).

One of the first targets on the young king's agenda was Ashkelon. Well fortified, and well connected with Egypt by sea, this stronghold put any Crusader attempt against Egypt in jeopardy. This Egyptian naval base had never been conquered by the Crusaders and continued to present an ongoing threat to the Latin Kingdom's southern border. Occupying Ashkelon would secure the lines of supply for any Crusader advance south into the Sinai.

After a long siege by both land and sea, the city was finally conquered in 1153. Now the entire coast of the Mediterranean Sea from Beirut to Gaza was in Christian hands. King Baldwin began to plan an assault further south into Egypt.

Before Crusader forces were able to move deeper into Egyptian territory, Baldwin had to deal with a new threat to the north: The Muslim Nur A Din. He, like his predecessor Zangi, had partially united the diverse clans of Islam, and had besieged and claimed the Syrian capital of Damascus.

The loss of Damascus (its only ally to the north) severely alarmed the Latin Kingdom. The situation at that border had become critical: instead of several small principalities, emirates and nomadic tribes occupied with intra-tribal squabbles, there was now a unified enemy, eager to war against the Crusaders and their European allies. However, Nur A Din was not yet able to devote his troops to a full-scale conflict, and the adversaries negotiated two years of peace.

When Baldwin 3rd died in 1163, his brother Amalric 1st was declared king and continued to set the kingdom's sights on Egypt. During Amalric's rule, several campaigns took the Christian knights across the Sinai Desert. On one occasion, Cairo was actually conquered and a Crusader garrison was stationed at the city gates. While the Shiite Muslims of Egypt did not desire the Latin Kingdom as master, they apparently preferred it to becoming the servants of the Sunnis Muslims united under Nur A Din – their mutual animosity having abated not at all.

Each Egypt campaign ended hastily when rumors arrived that a Syrian army was nearing the northern part of the Latin Kingdom. The Latin armies would halt operations and Amalric would reverse his march, leading his troops back across the desert to protect Jerusalem.

Despite such setbacks, Amalric still desired to press even further into Egypt. He convinced the Byzantine Emperor to ally with him in the north, where they both had a common interest: preventing Muslim encroachment. He wanted the Byzantine army to march on the Syrian border, and then to march with him to Egypt to secure his own flank. The Byzantine Emperor consented, but needed to conclude his army's current efforts in the Balkans before joining Amalric.

In October of 1168 – with the Byzantine army still tied up in the Balkans – the fourth and most significant of Amalric's forays into Egypt commenced. There was no sensible reason for it, as much of Egypt was already living peaceably under Latin control.

Amalric demanded two million gold coins from the Egyptians for the privilege of maintaining their autonomy. This was twenty times larger that the annual tribute currently being paid, and outside of Egypt's capability. By making such a demand, the Latin Kingdom moved from potential ally to obvious enemy. The desperate Egyptians appealed to the only power able to rescue them – Syria. Nur a Din marched his army south toward Egypt to clamp a vise on the Latin Kingdom.

With Egyptians on one side of him and the approaching Syrians on the other, Amalric found himself standing "between a rock and a hard place," the seemingly perpetual position of the inhabitants of the land of Israel. After two months of desert warfare, the Crusader army was compelled to withdraw, forfeiting any influence it had gained in Egypt and leaving the path open to Nur A Din.

The Syrian army went on to conquer Egypt, and Nur A Din's appointed governor – Saladin – rapidly established his authority in Egypt. Saladin was still technically subservient to Nur A Din, though his growing independence did worry the Syrian leader. (Saladin would eventually wrest control of Egypt for himself after Nur A Din's death, and become the founder of the Ayyubid dynasty.)

Jerusalem recognized that a united Syria and Egypt (resulting in enemy control of both interior borders and the related coastline) was dangerous, but the Latin Kingdom could do nothing to prevent it. However, perhaps due to each ruler's desire to limit the power of the other, Saladin and Nur A Din never joined forces against the Crusaders.

An uneasy peace endured until the Latin Kingdom made one last attempt to take Egypt a year later, this time with the help of Byzantium, which contributed more than two hundred manned ships and a large volume of supplies. Having a navy as well as land forces should have increased the chance of success, but once again the effort failed. Some blamed it on morale in the camp and the king's own lack of enthusiasm.

During five separate attempts, the Latin Kingdom had sought to subdue Egypt, but each attempt failed. In the process, war had been brought to the very borders of the kingdom. Egypt – a potential ally – became an enemy. Syria, already a strong enemy, marched into Egypt as deliverer, and cast its own net nearer and nearer the Latin Kingdom. Somehow a schism had also developed with the Byzantine Empire. It seemed the Latin

Kingdom would face the growing threat of Muslim expansion without any allies at all.

Saladin Presses In

Saladin seized the opportunity presented to him: he took Egyptian forces into Israel and conquered the Crusader post in Eilat. This greatly increased Saladin's own status, as it liberated Muslim pilgrims from the obligation to pay tribute to the Christians as they made pilgrimage to Mecca and Medina.

It seemed that Saladin's bid for more power in the Muslim world would eventually have to be decided in a face-off with Nur A Din, but the two never met in battle: Nur A Din died in Damascus in May of 1174. Two months later, Amalric died in Jerusalem. Saladin quickly maneuvered himself to take advantage of the resulting instability in both kingdoms.

Saladin first moved to establish control over Nur A Din's territory: he arrived in Damascus, proclaiming himself the guardian of Nur A Din's son. However, the northern Islamic countries considered Saladin an illegitimate ruler, and derisively referred to him as "the Kurd."

The situation was similar in the east: the Caliph of Baghdad, although he also wanted to drive out the Crusaders, would not openly stand behind Saladin. The diverse and clannish factions of the Muslim world seemed unable to rally behind one leader no matter what the cause.

Damascus had accepted Saladin (perhaps they had little choice upon his arrival), but many of the other walled cities in Syria closed their gates. The leaders of Aleppo, strongly opposed to Saladin, led the attempt to unite all of Syria against him.

Even though already five times a failure, The Crusaders saw this Muslim dispute as a golden opportunity: with Saladin's presence and attention in Syria, Egypt lay unprotected. A regiment of knights led by Philip, Count of Flanders had recently arrived from Europe to reinforce the kingdom. To further enhance the odds, matters had been patched up with Byzantium and its navy was again available to the Crusader kingdom. King Baldwin 4th was determined to lead another attack on Egypt.

Unfortunately for the Christians, the spirit of solidarity that had typified the first decades of the Latin presence in the Orient had disappeared. Count Philip had apparently come to the Holy Land with his own agenda, and refused to join Baldwin, saying he was there only as a pilgrim. (Some say his real intent was to marry his vassals to the Latin Kingdom's royal princesses.)

Saladin rushed back to Egypt to organize its defense. Since the Christian attack was first delayed and then canceled, he had time to go on the offensive: In mid-November, 1177, the Egyptian army crossed the Sinai desert and stood at the gates of Gaza. A general mobilization was declared while King Baldwin and most of the army rode to the fortified city of Ashekelon, several miles north of Gaza.

Other Christian forces, rushing to join the king, were destroyed on the way south. With the main body of the Latin army in Ashkelon, the rest of the kingdom was unprotected. Muslim troops rode through the land, attacking and pillaging smaller towns and villages. With nothing to stop it, the Muslim army could now advance into the hill country and cut off the roads leading into Jerusalem.

Fortunately for the Latins, Saladin had left no one in the area of Ashkelon to monitor Baldwin's moves, and the Crusader army was able to leave Ashkelon, pick up additional troops from small fortresses along the way, and ride rapidly along the coast without arousing Muslim alarm.

Flanking thc Muslim forces, Baldwin's troops fell on them near Gezer, on the highway to Jerusalem. The Muslim ranks, taken by surprise, were scattered – and hurriedly retreated towards Egypt. Saladin barely managed to escape.

November 25, 1177, the day of Saladin's defeat, was a day of shame on the Muslim calendar for years to come. Saladin had suffered his worst defeat in over 35 years of military action. The great Christian victory (after five defeats) was mainly of value to the army's morale, as it did not change the balance of power or the political situation in the region.

King Baldwin did not allow himself to be blinded by the unexpected success. Unified Muslim forces now encircled the Latin Kingdom, and he recognized that no longer would traditional military campaigns be able to protect the land. In order to survive, the resources of the kingdom had to be applied instead to the continued fortification of cities and strongholds.

The famous "King's Highway," a major trade route, traversed the Latin Kingdom. Through that territory, richly laden caravans, as well as hundreds of thousands of Muslim pilgrims, made their way to the Arabian Peninsula. It was crucial for Saladin to eliminate danger to Muslims traveling in either direction. Since the Crusader kingdom had done much to intensify its grip in that area (numerous well-supplied and well-manned fortresses covered the land), Saladin eventually recognized that this safety could not be obtained by force. In 1180, after a string of small skirmishes between the Crusaders princes and Turkish invaders, Saladin and Baldwin 4th agreed to a truce.

Raynald the Pirate

The truce allowed the protected flow of commerce and Muslim pilgrims through the heavily fortified Crusader territory. The truce only lasted a year, though, and was violated – against the king's will and the kingdom's interest – by the Baron of the Trans-Jordan, Raynald of Châtillon.

Desiring to avail himself of the traveling riches, Raynald attacked a Muslim pilgrims' convoy. Isolated by his geographic location, Raynald undoubtedly felt that this action would neither be severely challenged nor reap drastic consequences from his own king. He was right on both counts.

Raynald's act is a classic example of the lack of discipline among the Latin Barons. They formally submitted to the king's authority when knighted, but once obtaining that position, some acted with an unwelcome degree of independence. It was almost impossible for the king to exercise his will over his knights, especially those in the more remote areas of the kingdom. This was Baldwin's excuse for Raynald's action – his own inability to control it.

The broken truce transformed Saladin once again into a powerful enemy. The Crusaders, now with a reduced treasury and weaker army, were forced to plan their moves carefully and practice restraint. On the other hand, Saladin's resources were almost unlimited. He could exert ongoing pressure along the borders, with the luxury of replacing his troops periodically. In this game of cat and mouse, Saladin was clearly the cat. Saladin could not mount a full-scale attack only because some of his attention was taken up with fellow Muslims unhappy with his own growing power.

As Saladin dealt with internal opposition, the initiative fell once again into Crusader hands. Several raids were made into the rural areas around Damascus. Some minor Christian strongholds, recently taken by Saladin, were reclaimed. Once again the Christians were able to manipulate the Muslim clan leaders into fighting amongst themselves.

Raynald continued to cause trouble: He ordered five ships to be constructed in his fortress in the desert so that he could invade the Arabian Peninsula by sea and conquer Medina. The parts were carried on camels to the Red Sea and assembled there, where the ships then set sail. The subsequent raid on the coastal road, flooded with pilgrims and laden caravans, shook the Muslim world: Christian infidels were marching through Hijaz, the very cradle of Islam. This was intolerable, and by Saladin's orders, a force was sent from Egypt to pursue and kill all the participants in the raid.

Meanwhile, Saladin's own troubles continued. Aleppo had surrendered to him on June 12, 1183, but Mosul in Iraq still refused to join with him, and the rising tally of Muslim opponents was beginning to erode Saladin's support, even among those who were already his. The one thing that might unite the Muslims under his leadership was a Jihad – the Muslim holy war.

Dissention in the Latin Kingdom

In the Latin Kingdom things were getting worse: Baldwin 4th' on his deathbed, crowned his five-year-old nephew as King of Jerusalem. Guy De Lusignan, Baldwin's brother-in-law (the expected heir and the commander of the army) then fled to his fortress in Ashkelon. The court was now divided between Guy's followers and those who sided with the new child king.

The dissonance in the court distracted the kingdom from making preparations for a possible war. The young king died in

1186 at only the age of seven, and Guy and a new adult rival – Count Raymond of Galilee – raced for the throne, hurrying to be the first to arrive in Jerusalem.

On July 20, 1186, Guy De Lusignan was crowned King of Jerusalem in the Church of the Holy Sepulcher. The kingdom was still divided, however. The powerful Knights Templar supported Guy and so did the city's Patriarch, but some of the Barons refused to offer their allegiance to the new king; they believed he had had gained his position only through marriage – and illegally at that.

This lack of agreement among the barons and other leadership certainly contributed to the downfall of the first Latin Kingdom. When clever judgment was needed, as well as unity and discipline, suspicion, division, and animosity prevailed instead.

The First Kingdom Falls

King Guy's ability to lead the kingdom was tested less than a year later, when Saladin attacked in June of 1187. This new strike was in keeping with his prevailing strategy: constant pressure on the Latin Kingdom's borders. Even though the Muslim force was large, there was no reason to believe that the campaign would be anything more than the usual skirmish.

When Saladin conquered Tiberias, the royal Latin council convened and decided not to immediately counter with an offensive. Experience had proven that the Muslim army could be effective for a time, but its determination waned if weeks passed without significant progress: the Muslim soldiers would run low on both supplies and motivation, and eventually disperse across the countryside. So the Crusader army remained camped at the springs of Zippori in central Galilee, content to "wait and see."

That night, soon after the decision had been made, Gerard de Richfort, the commander of the Knights Templar, arrived at the camp and stormed into King Guy's tent. He expressed his disgust at the council's decision and declared that the Crusader army would be disgraced if it did not immediately move to liberate Tiberias, which stood only a few miles away. His argument was persuasive, the council reversed its decision, and at dawn on Friday, July 3, 1187, the Latin army marched toward Tiberias.

This proved a costly error. All of the kingdom's forces were now concentrated in one place, facing a superior number of Muslim troops. Even their method of advancement worked against them: the Latin soldiers, still fighting in the tradition of medieval armies, marched very slowly in tight formation. Against the Muslims, such a rigid arrangement was a liability. The Muslim archers were able to constantly needle the rearguard and provoke the ranks to confusion.

The Muslims set fire to the dry vegetation in the valley surrounding the battlefield. This, added to the debilitating heat and the constant barrage of arrows, took a heavy toll on the Latins, who eventually sought not to win the battle but simply to escape the carnage. Only one regiment managed to flee, while the others climbed one of the hills nearby – the Horns of Hittin. Only a day later, on Saturday, July 4 1187, the remaining soldiers, a majority of the entire Latin army, surrendered to Saladin's forces.

Convoys of Christian prisoners of war began to make their way to Damascus. Both King Guy and Raynald, the pirate of the Trans-Jordan, had been captured. Saladin spared King Guy's life but beheaded Raynald with a blow from his own sword – saying death was necessary payment for Raynald's treachery and deceit in violating the treaty.

Massive Crusader fortresses still dotted the landscape, but with most of the knights in Damascus as prisoners of war, Saladin's forces had little trouble subduing the rest of the kingdom. The scattered strongholds fell one by one, and the few that remained independent could only hope for swift European intervention. By mid-September, the Muslim army had surrounded Jerusalem. The siege lasted only three weeks and then the city, without any warriors to defend it and with no hope of immediate help, opened its gates to Saladin.

Jerusalem, the capital of the Christian kingdom, was once again in Muslim hands. The crescent replaced the cross above the Dome of the Rock, and the banner of Islam again snapped proudly in the wind that scoured Jerusalem's walls.

14

The Second Latin Kingdom
c. 1189 - 1254

The Third or Kings' Crusade

Europe, unable to prevent the destruction of the Latin Kingdom, nonetheless responded quickly, initiating what became known as the Third Crusade. The mighty kings of Europe, leading professional armies, made their way to the Holy Land. The German Emperor Frederick 1st 'raveled overland with one hundred thousand men. It was an imposing army with a good chance of recapturing the Holy Land and reestablishing the Latin Kingdom.

Soon after this, King Philip of France and Richard the Lion Hearted (newly King of England) followed; but only after many discussions and much negotiation. Both swore an oath that for the duration of the Crusade they would forgo acts of aggression in Europe. Only then did either king dare to leave his country.

As those in Europe were preparing for the journey, the defeated King Guy, who had been released by Saladin, lost no time in gathering what remained of his army. He could no longer claim royal authority to lead and did not enjoy full loyalty; many blamed him for the final defeat. Nevertheless, there were a number of people hiding in Galilee and other places who answered his call.

The first ships with reinforcements from Europe had arrived by this time, and Guy recruited these men for his army. In the summer of 1189, the Crusader forces set up camp outside the walls of the port city of Acre. Soon after, Saladin's forces encircled the Crusader camp. This unusual situation lasted three long years: themselves surrounded by the Muslim army, the Crusaders besieged Acre, waiting for reinforcements from Europe. Those loyal to the Crusader cause continued to make their way gradually to the area. The Crusader army was constantly growing, but it was not yet strong enough to attack Acre.

In Europe, things were also moving slowly. The German army had scattered after Emperor Frederick 1st drowned while crossing a river in Asia Minor, and only a fraction of the original German force made it as far as Acre. At the end of April 1191, the French and English armies arrived and the battle finally commenced. The city fell three months later. Saladin's troops stood nearby, powerless to alter the outcome.

While a significant victory, Acre was still only a bridgehead. There was much more to do if the Latin Kingdom was to be restored. King Philip left for home; Richard the Lionhearted led the armies of the Third Crusade further south.

Richard's campaign was of little success. Some of the coastal cities were taken but Jerusalem was not; his armies never even made the attempt. Nevertheless, after negotiations with Saladin on September 2, 1192, the Muslims recognized the existence of a new Latin Kingdom. Although Jerusalem, Bethlehem, Nazareth and other Christian holy sites were not included within the new kingdom's borders, Christian pilgrims would still be allowed to visit some of them.

Henry of Champagne was named as ruler of the second Latin Kingdom. King Guy, the last monarch of the first kingdom, became king of the Isle of Cyprus, which had been conquered by Richard the Lion Hearted as he had made his way to Acre.

Because the new Crusade had been in essence a European military operation, it did not bring people with it who would stay and inhabit the hard-won areas. The soldiers came to fulfill their oath, not to live in the land. The sparse settlement made the kingdom that much harder to defend. The small size of the kingdom – the coastline between Tyre and Joppa – was also a continual concern.

Fortunately for the new small kingdom, Saladin, who by charismatic leadership and force of will had united the Arab world, died in March of 1193. Soon, the Ayyubid Empire began to disintegrate. Old schisms resurfaced, despite the fact that Saladin's successors were his own sons.

King Henry and his men were careful not to intervene in Muslim affairs. Their strategy was simple: to wait patiently until more Christian forces arrived, while continuing to build up the kingdom and strengthen the monarchy. King Henry died in 1197 and was succeeded by Amalric 2nd, the older brother of Guy de Lusignan.

On July 1, 1198, a truce was signed between the Latin Kingdom and Damascus, now ruled by El Adil (Saladin's brother). It was renewed for five years in 1204.

The Fourth Crusade

In Europe, the pure motives behind Crusade fever had become diluted, and soon it seemed that whomever Western Europe regarded as an enemy became the target of a Crusade. What came to be called the Fourth Crusade did not truly deserve the title. It was indeed a military journey, but the objective was not the protection or recovery of holy sites or the defeat of the heathen – this time the objective was Byzantium.

On April 13, 1204, Latin forces conquered the Byzantine capital of Constantinople, and for nearly 50 years, Westerners ruled the Eastern Christian world. The new kingdom was named The Latin Empire, and its new emperor invited any knight who wanted land and provisions to come and reside in Byzantine territory. Hundreds left the Latin Kingdom, which was already suffering from a severe shortage of manpower.

European knights and kings continued to come to the Orient, but for many of them, the desire for personal gain outweighed religious motivation. They were careful not to take risks and not to be remembered as those who had failed. Such men came for a limited time, conducted limited operations and returned home with the title "Crusader" to enhance their reputations. Not surprisingly, the Latin Kingdom benefited little through any of these ventures.

The Fifth Crusade

For example, during the Fifth Crusade in 1219, when a Crusader army had invaded deep into Egypt, the Egyptian Sultan was willing (in return for a ceasefire) to give up all the land between the Jordan River and the Mediterranean Sea. Even though the current Latin king (John of Brienne) was enthusiastic, the European leaders of the Crusade rejected the offer – their desire was to establish reputations on the battlefield, not at the negotiation table. The chance for an advantageous peace was lost, refused by men who did not have to live under the consequences of that refusal. The Egyptian Sultan El Kamil (a nephew of Saladin) eventually defeated the Crusader forces and the eight-year truce that followed was on his terms.

A New King and the Sixth Crusade

Hope for the renewed kingdom surged again when, while King John was visiting Europe in 1223, he offered his ten-year-old daughter Isabel (his heir) as bride to the German Emperor, Frederick 2nd.

Fredrick's acceptance of Isabel was conditional upon King John's willingness to give him the throne of the Latin Kingdom. The king reluctantly agreed, and the Latin barons were required now to accept Frederick as their master. Frederick had committed himself as a Crusader long before, however, his journey to the Holy Land had been postponed repeatedly; some thought due to Frederick's reluctance rather than any real hindrance. Finally, on September 8, 1227, after years of hesitation, Frederick boarded his flagship and his huge fleet slowly left Italy. Only three days later, Frederick announced he was ill and aborted the journey.

Incensed and exasperated, the Pope (Gregory IXth) excommunicated the German emperor. However, before leaving Italy, Frederick had already made an impact in the east: exploiting the turmoil within the Ayyubid Empire, he had brokered his own treaty with Egypt.

El Kamil in Egypt was concerned about a possible war with his relatives ruling Syria and Mesopotamia. He was also weary of disputes with the Christians. Regarding the Latin Kingdom as a useful obstruction between Egypt and Syria, he had promised in the treaty to give land to Frederick – but it was not his to dispose of. El Muatham (the Sultan of Damascus and El Kamil's uncle) ruled the area.

Just before Frederick's forces were ready to leave Italy once again, El Muatham of Syria died. Since his successor was young and inexperienced, and presumably less of a threat, Egypt's El Kamil had second thoughts about the treaty. When Frederick landed on the shores of Tripoli in September of 1228, he also decided to evaluate the new circumstances before proceeding. A busy correspondence began while the Crusader army, thousands of pilgrims, and the local aristocracy waited for orders to advance towards Jerusalem.

Frederick and El Kamil negotiated a new agreement in February 1229. What the previous Crusades had failed to accomplish, Frederick did without a battle. He had demonstrated his skills as a negotiator, if not as a general.

Since the Church had excommunicated Frederick, it was quick to criticize him and accused him of betrayal in regards to the treaty, claiming that it gave Frederick some advantage but ignored the needs of the kingdom. In the agreement, the Christians had gained some territory. The most important acquisitions were Bethlehem and Jerusalem. The holy city was transferred to the Christians; however, the Muslims kept the right to worship on Temple Mount. Despite the return of several holy sites to the Latin Kingdom's control, the papal delegate in Acre was incensed that the treaty did not even mention the Church.

Frederick's wife Isabel had died only a week after giving birth to a son, the legitimate heir to the throne. But until the boy (Conrad) turned 15, Frederick, as the queen's husband, was the de facto king of Jerusalem. A month after the new treaty was signed a column of soldiers (with Frederick in its midst) hiked the mountains of Judea and entered Jerusalem through an opening in its ruined walls. The next day, after assuming control of the city, Frederick entered the Church of the Holy Sepulcher. He took the crown that stood on the altar and placed it on his head. There was no ceremony nor were there any Papal representatives present.

A few hours later, the Latin archbishop of Caesarea appeared in Jerusalem, banning the city and everyone in it who would dare to accept the excommunicated Frederick as king. The churches that had opened just the day before were closed, and thousands of pilgrims left the city in order to escape the church's ban. Within two months (May 1229) a disgusted Frederick left Jerusalem, traveled to Acre to join his fleet, and sailed for Europe. He left behind him a large territory, defensible only as long as the Muslims respected the recent treaty.

Frederick had taken the infant heir back with him and left a German nobleman as his regent. The regent's authority was not recognized by the citizens of the land, but only by visiting Europeans. This added to the internal controversy and the hostilities that already existed, as the Crusader barons found themselves constantly quarrelling over legal issues and matters of state.

The Barons' Crusade

A short time later back in Italy, Frederick waged and won a war against the Papal army. In 1230, due to this victory, Pope Gregory IX officially recognized Frederick's position as King of Jerusalem and reversed his excommunication. Frederick again set sail for the Latin Kingdom, determined to protect his interests there. On September 1, 1239, this "Barons' Crusade" arrived at Acre. It was an impressive army, numbering thousands of soldiers and fifteen hundred knights.

Upon arrival, the army's commander, Thibault of Champagne, met with the local leaders to try and pinpoint the goals of the Crusade. It seems incredible that thousands of people had crossed the Great Sea without a clear idea of what they intended to do or of the needs of the people they seemingly came to rescue. The peace of a decade earlier was still in place. Without a clear agenda, this Barons' Crusade seemed more a threat to the Kingdom than a necessary intervention.

After two months camped outside Acre, the army headed south on November 2, 1239. The plan was to conquer and fortify Ashkelon, then attack Damascus to the north.

While the Crusader army was marching to Ashkelon, its French knights came to believe the army's goals were too limited and decided to leave the main force and advance directly into Egypt. Disregarding Thibault's request to remain, they crossed the border into Egypt and approached Gaza. The next morning, just before dawn, the renegade knights halted in a shallow valley surrounded by low sand dunes. Muslim forces, which had been shadowing them undetected, attacked.

In the deep sand, the Crusader horses could hardly move and the French knights fell one by one. Only a few were able to escape the carnage, breaking through the Muslim lines to warn the main Crusader camp; however, the defeat was so devastating that it brought an end to the Crusade and severely demoralized the soldiers. The Muslim victors decapitated the fallen knights and strung their heads like beads along the walls of Cairo.

Unnerved and angry, Thibault returned to Acre. While he paused there, an unexpected advantage fell to his hands: the Sultan of Damascus, a sworn enemy of his Muslim brethren in Egypt, saw in the frustrated Crusader forces a potential ally.

Thibault signed a treaty with Damascus, adding to the Latin Kingdom's territory despite the failure of the recent Crusade. Satisfied with this achievement, Thibault left the Levant only two weeks before another Christian army led by Richard of Cornwell (the brother of King Henry 3rd of England) landed on the same shores in September 1240.

This fresh Christian army in Israel was enough to make the Sultan of Damascus newly nervous. He made Richard a generous offer, and once again, without wars and costly heroics, the Latin Kingdom improved its situation significantly. The new borders were defendable. In addition to what Thibault had gained, the area south of Jerusalem was added to the kingdom and part of inland Galilee as well. No longer mere enclaves connected by narrow land corridors, the kingdom was now a continuous strip along the coast uninterrupted by Muslim territories. The local leaders were jubilant. It was indeed a strategic victory; however, establishing a country's borders on paper was meaningless if the land didn't contain settlers, churches, and fortifications.

Outside resources poured into the impoverished country to fund building projects along the Crusader-Egyptian border. In the heart of Galilee, the stronghold of Safed became a massive fortress. Slowly, the walls of Jerusalem were repaired and building projects were initiated in Ashkelon and Joppa. It seemed as though the war-torn kingdom had received a new lease on life; but amidst the peace and prosperity a new threat surged in from the desert.

The Turks

In 1219, the Shah of Persia had murdered Mongol diplomats who had been sent to him by Genghis Khan. In retaliation, two hundred thousand Mongol warriors invaded Central Asia, overrunning such cities as Bukhara and Samarkand (in modern Uzbekistan). The area became part of the Mongol Empire, and many Turks and other peoples fled to escape Mongol rule.

Over the next few decades, multitudes of displaced Turks moved into the Middle East and allied themselves with Egypt. Temporarily settled along the Middle Euphrates River, the Turks accepted the invitation of Sultan As-Salih (this prodigal son of El Kamil had overthrown his brother in 1240 to seize control of Egypt) to invade Crusader territory and win back the land El

Kamil had given away. The Turks were without a country but still warriors - and probably hoped to prove the courage and ferocity that had done them little good against the Mongols.

The Turks stormed through the Latin Kingdom. They were not equipped to lay siege and so sought vulnerable targets: Jerusalem, with her protective walls still in a state of reconstruction, was attacked in July of 1244. The city repelled the first attempt, but eventually ceded the city to the Turks. A few days later, under a protective umbrella of knights, some seven thousand people left the city and fled to Joppa. This exodus of Jerusalem's Christian inhabitants ended fifteen years of Christian occupation in Jerusalem, made possible by the treaty negotiated by Frederick the 2nd·

Meanwhile, as per the recent agreement between Damascus and the Latin Kingdom, an unusual coalition of Syrians and Crusaders was making final arrangements to invade Egypt. On October 4 of the same year, the Crusader army left Acre, heading south to join with Syrian forces at Ashkelon. It was the largest concentration of Christian forces since the defeat at Hittin. Ten thousand infantry accompanied more than two thousand Christian knights. It was the first time in many years that the fragmented kingdom had drawn together in such an organized effort.

On October 17, 1244, the battle known as "Hittin 2" was engaged. The Egyptian army inflicted terrible losses on the coalition, and only about a hundred knights survived the slaughter. The achievements of the previous 15 years, all the efforts of Frederick, Thibault, and Richard of Cornwell were nullified in a single battle.

Europe finally began to show signs of exhaustion from the Crusades. The papacy was compelled to face the fact that even with an enormous investment of resources and human lives,

European efforts in the east had borne little fruit. This fatigue signaled the eventual end of the second Latin Kingdom, but the Europeans weren't quite finished yet.

The Seventh Crusade

Fortunately for the Latin Kingdom, Louis 9th of France was interested in preserving the Holy Land. Everything in Louis' personality and education had prepared him to be the ultimate Crusader: his chivalry and piety mirrored the Crusader ideal. You might say King Louis 9th was a perfect fit as the man who would lead the last significant Crusade in the Levant.

His Crusade was perhaps the best organized of them all. Carefully defining its goals, he decided to take the army into Egypt. He believed that by defeating Egypt (the Latin Kingdom's strongest adversary) he could secure the Holy Land. The German Frederick 2nd (father of the absent Latin child king Conrad II) offered to help. In return, Louis promised that all conquered countries would be annexed to the Latin Kingdom's territory. (Frederick was again at odds with the papacy, due to his continual attempts to wrest power from the church. Pope Innocent IV had formally removed him from the German throne in 1245, and Frederick's willingness to help Louis was probably in the hopes that his son and heir would gain a kingdom for them both.)

Only those deemed beneficial to the quest were allowed to join the camp, and drinking, gambling and other hedonistic activities were strictly prohibited. Undoubtedly, such requirements pleased the Pope, but the church was barely involved in the Crusade. King Louis set the requirements.

A fleet two thousand ships strong carried food and other supplies to the island of Cyprus where the vast army was based. The fleet arrived in September of 1248. Wisely, the king of France spent the winter making peace with and creating alliances among the various Christian parties in the region. He was determined not to repeat the mistakes of those who had preceded him.

In May of 1249, King Louis' army headed south to the shores of Egypt. On June 4, the French forces landed by Damietta. The Muslim forces awaiting them there were easily scattered, and the city fell later that day. However, instead of pressing the advantage and marching on into the heart of Egypt before the Nile flood season, the Christian army halted its advance for nearly six months.

The delay served the Egyptians well: they were able to expand and train their armies, and gather allies from other parts of the Muslim world.

After six months of inactivity, the Crusaders left Damietta and headed into the flooded area of the Nile. That part of Egypt, covered by a network of canals and streams as well as irrigation facilities and water reservoirs, was a soggy morass that brought the Crusader army to a halt, its horses unable to move through the sludge.

Two days after the Christian army started this advance, the Egyptian Sultan (As-Salih) died. His widow kept his death a secret, and she took command of the army while her son made his way back to Egypt. The Crusaders, still trapped in the sodden floodplains of the Nile, were helpless against the Muslim archers and artillery, which took a terrible toll on both the knights and their horses. After several weeks, when the food had run out and corpses had poisoned the water, the Crusaders retreated hurriedly to Damietta. When King Louis' life was threatened by disease, the army surrendered. The king was taken to Cairo as a prisoner of war.

Egypt negotiated a settlement, exacting compensation from the Crusader army in exchange for King Louis. Those negotiations concluded on May 6, 1250. Two days later he was on his way to Acre. Apparently, the French king was in no hurry to return to France. Louis stayed in the Levant for another five years. He dedicated his time to building and fortifying the coastal cities of the Latin Kingdom, scarcely noting the ebb and flow of fierce Muslim infighting all around him. Finally in April of 1254, Louis sailed for home, leaving behind him a small kingdom without a king.

The Seventh Crusade was the last substantial effort that Europe made to maintain its Christian grip on the Holy Land. By the time King Louis left for France, the Latin Kingdom existed in name only.

15

The Mamluks
c. 1291-1516

Delivered from the Mongols

The Latin Kingdom was no longer in control of its own destiny. The Crusader armies had sailed home, and most of the great fortresses now lay in abandoned heaps. After Egypt had regained Jerusalem via the Turks, the few other remaining Latin principalities stood virtually alone and unprotected. To add to the tension, a new enemy threatened, intent upon using Israel as a steppingstone to Egypt.

Scything into the Middle East, Mongol warriors had by this time cut a swath to the northern border of Israel, devastating Syria along the way. Their mode of warfare was absolute and humiliating destruction if their offer of a peaceful surrender was refused. After word of their atrocities spread, it was the rare monarch who faced the Mongol threat and did not capitulate. The Mongol leader of this campaign (Hulagu Khan, the grandson of Genghis Khan) had written to Qutuz, the Mamluk leader of Egypt (the Mamluks had seized power from the Abbasid dynasty) and invited him to surrender or face the consequences.

In reply, Qutuz killed the Mongol couriers, hung their heads on the gates of Cairo, and sped north to Israel with his army.

Initially, the Latin Kingdom had thought to align itself with the Mongols against Egypt, reasoning that it was only a matter of time before the Mongols destroyed them both; but the Pope forbade the alliance and the Latin Kingdom instead allowed unhindered passage to the Egyptian army, promising not to inform the Mongols of Egyptian troop movements. In return, the Mamluk leaders of Egypt essentially saved Israel from annihilation.

In an historic conflict on Friday, September 3, 1260, the Mamluks met the Mongols on the eastern plains of Jezreel in northern Israel, in the battle of Ain Jalut. Baybars, the man who would destroy the Latin Kingdom, was the Mamluk commander of the Egyptian army. The battle's outcome would determine the destiny of the Middle East for centuries.

The Mongol army, though still quite large, was not at full force: Hulagu Khan had returned home at the death of his brother in order to prevent a military coup, and he had taken a portion of the army with him. By noon, it was obvious that the Mongols had experienced their first major defeat. They fled north towards Damascus and Aleppo. It was an important defeat historically for the Mongols, in that it marked the first time they were never able to return and avenge their loss.

The victorious Mamluk army headed back to Egypt and while on the way, Baybars assassinated Qutuz and seized the sultanate – apparently because Qutuz, years before, had murdered his friend.

Now fully in control in Israel, the new Mamluk regime busily prepared the territory against future Mongol attack. An efficient road system was constructed, and fortresses that the Muslims had destroyed a few years earlier were rebuilt, providing a stronger line of defense. A weak Crusader kingdom continued to exist, but only because Baybars' energies were consumed with the possible Mongol threat. When the Mongol forces proved mostly inactive, the huge Muslim army that had been concentrated in Palestine was eventually mobilized to attack the remaining Latin principalities. Baybars was a faithful student of previous Egyptian sultans. He understood that the most efficient way to defeat the Christians was to level everything to the ground. He did not hesitate to do so. Caesarea, one of the jewels of the Latin Kingdom, fortified by Louis 9th °nly a decade before, was the first to fall, on March 5, 1265.

The year 1266 brought more disaster: the fortress of Safed in upper Galilee, one of the largest in the kingdom, was attacked. Six weeks of siege caused little damage to its massive walls and both camps were exhausted. The Muslim victory came only when Baybars craftily stated that his quarrel was with the knights and not with the ordinary soldiers: he offered asylum to the commoners, demanding full surrender from the knights.

The common soldiers, all of them Christians from the eastern churches who considered themselves poorly treated by the Latin knights, surrendered to Baybars. Thus the fortress of Safed, and all of Galilee with it, fell on June 23, 1266. The Crusader knights, instead of receiving safe passage home as Baybars had promised, were slaughtered.

Baybars had enough manpower to engage the scattered Christian troops simultaneously and Joppa fell next. Mamluk troops devastated the principality of Antioch in May of 1268. The Crusader kingdom was entirely in Mamluk control; it only remained for the last of the Christians to be forced from the land.

The Eighth Crusade

France's King Louis 9th made one more attempt to regain the Holy Land for the Church. He landed on the African coast in July of 1270, but died in August. His brother Charles of Anjou took command of the troops. The Crusaders besieged Tunis, but abandoned the attempt in October.

The Ninth Crusade

While Charles and his forces were still in Africa, the crown prince Edward 1st of England arrived at the port city of Acre in his own attempt to reclaim Israel. The Mamluks under Baybars had completely and brutally subdued the Holy Land, and Edward hoped to engage the assistance of the Mongols in his efforts to turn back the tide. Before he had arrived, a busy exchange of letters had made its way between Prince Edward and the Mongol court. Edward hoped to attack the Muslim forces from Acre while the Mongols struck concurrently from the east.

While planning the Ninth Crusade, he was shocked to learn that the Venetians in Acre were trading with the Muslims, even as the Muslims were attempting to destroy the city. it was a painful introduction to the disunity that prevailed. Each party attended to its own concerns regardless of what was best for the disintegrating kingdom.

While Edward enjoyed some success against the Mamluks, word reached him in 1272 that his father had died. He eventually negotiated a treaty with Baybars and sailed home in April of 1272 to be crowned King of England. The Ninth Crusade is considered the last of the medieval Crusades. The final curtain was coming down on the Holy Land.

The Kingdom Falls

Baybars died in the summer of 1277 and a new sultan seized the throne – Qalawoon, who took the title Al-Mansur. In 1282, ten years of ceasefire in Israel came to an end and hostilities began anew. In April of 1289, after six weeks of siege, the earldom of Tripoli fell. The destruction that followed virtually erased the city from the face of the earth.

At the end of 1289, only a few Christians were left along the eastern shores of the Mediterranean. Any movement between coastal cities had to be made by sea, since the Muslims dominated the highways. Cyprus, off the coast, was somewhat safe from attack due to its position. Soon it offered the only place to flee.

The Muslims dedicated the following year, 1290, to the removal of all Christians from the land. Calls for Jihad once again rang through the mosques. A large army was deploying in the plains outside of Acre, and huge cedar logs were brought from the mountains of Lebanon to build mobile towers.

Even the death of Al Mansur stopped the work for only a short time: his son El Ashraf carried on without losing momentum. By April of 1291, the Muslim army was ready. Under covering fire from the Muslim artillery, the diggers advanced towards the moat, shielded by wooden walls. Soil and rock were shoveled in, preparing a path for the mobile towers, from where the Muslim troops would assail the walls of the city.

The Crusaders, on the edge of destruction, fought heroically. Shoulder to shoulder, completely united for the first time in years, the citizens of Acre held off the Muslim forces. Despite their bravery and courage, however, the outcome was inevitable.

On May 18, 1291, forty-four days after the siege commenced, the city fell. The last stronghold in the city, held by the Knights

Templar, was quickly evacuated. The building was set on fire almost immediately, and in the light of the flames, several ships could be seen, carrying the remnants of the Latin Kingdom towards Cyprus. On board, gazing at the ruined city that had been their capital for a century, stood those knights – never to return again.

On August 14, 1291, the last Crusader fortress was abandoned and yielded to the Muslims. The Latin Kingdom was finally dead.

The new Mamluk masters wanted to discourage any future efforts by Western Europe to conduct another Crusade in the Holy Land, so they ravaged the coastal cities and demolished everything that could be useful in such an attempt. They closed up the deep harbors by filling them in with stones from tumbled-down city walls. The ruins of other once-thriving cities and irrigation systems scarred the inland landscape, and the rich farmland that had previously fed the nation now lay depleted and barren.

Israel was devastated. Seven hundred years would pass before Jewish pioneers would build new towns and cities and drain the swampy land so that rich harvests could be claimed again.

Since the Crusaders were no longer a possible menace, and the chance of another Crusade was slim, the Mamluks dedicated their resources to establishing themselves in the Muslim sphere. They turned to readdress an old threat: the Mongols.

Soon after the Mongol defeat of Baghdad in 1258, many Mongols had converted to Islam, creating a Muslim Mongol kingdom east of the Euphrates. The Mamluks were wary of this kingdom. They were also concerned about Armenia, the only significant Christian kingdom in the area, which had allied with the Mongols in the hopes of obtaining control of the Christian holy sites in Israel.

The main goal of the Mamluks was to establish protection along the Euphrates River (a natural feature easy to protect) in order to defend the kingdom against a Mongol advance. In order to do so, the various rival emirates in Northern Syria had to first achieve some degree of unity.

Once that was accomplished, securing the land connection between the two Mamluk territories (Egypt and Syria) was crucial. Established army posts and a good road system would guarantee the flow of commodities and the safety of pilgrims on their way to the Hajj in Mecca or Medina. The Mamluk Empire dedicated itself to these projects. Israel benefited tremendously from the trade caravans and the pilgrims traveling through on the improved and fortified highways.

Though the road system was safe and efficient, the Mamluks had no navy. While Western Europe was no longer a threat, it was feared that the island kingdom of Cyprus might make an attempt to reclaim Israel. To address this possible threat by sea, the Mamluks turned to European city-states such as Venice, Genoa, and Pisa, which for the right price were willing to establish naval bases in Muslim territory.

The Mamluk Empire eventually dominated the caravan trade between east and west. Through its protected road system, law and order were established in an environment that for decades had been dangerous to travelers and indefensible due to the lack of cooperation among the many peoples of the land. The Mamluks, in many ways outsiders even among the Muslims, had succeeded where many others had failed.

Who Were They?

Who were the Mamluks and what made them such efficient and capable rulers?

With the rapid expansion of Islam during the seventh and the eighth centuries, Islam had penetrated to the Asian wilderness, where Barbarian nomads had migrated from Asia and Mongolia. The land the nomads wandered was of no value to the Muslims, but the people were: the Mamluks were exceptionally hardy and accustomed to challenging living conditions. These qualities made them excellent potential soldiers, and the Egyptian armies were constantly in need of fresh recruits.

Mamluk children were captured and brought to Egypt as slaves, tutored in Islam, and then the males were trained as soldiers. Once training was over, they were released from slavery and considered fully Muslim.

The Egyptian authorities were very careful to restrict the numbers of Mamluk slaves one master could have, and the total number of Mamluks in the kingdom. Many were grateful to their masters and to Islam, and became useful additions to Muslim society. Without families nearby, their loyalties were to their masters and to Egypt.

The Mamluks became the elite of Muslim warriors, dedicated in their service to Islam and Egypt. While in Syria numerous emirs continued to fight against each other, Egypt stayed relatively calm and more or less united under one ruler. Egypt's rulers used the Mamluk warriors to reinforce their authority, and the Mamluks themselves garnered power in this capacity. Some in Egypt were uneasy at the growing strength of the Mamluks, since they were in fact aliens in the land. On the other hand, it was widely acknowledged that the Mamluk warriors had repeatedly saved Egypt from its enemies.

During 1249, while the Crusader army of King Louis 9th was advancing into Egyptian territory, the Egyptian Sultan As-Salih of Egypt had died. The crown prince, away in Syria, immediately set out for Egypt, but in the meantime the advancing Crusader army

Crusader army highlighted the urgent need of a commander for the Egyptian forces; a Mamluk was appointed. When the crown prince arrived, the Mamluks assassinated him. The new Mamluk sultan had already married the widow of the late ruler, and so the coup was not severely challenged. As much as the Egyptian aristocracy disapproved, they also had to admit that it was essentially Mamluk skill, bravery and determination that had delivered Egypt from a Crusader victory.

Since the Mamluks did not mingle with Egyptian society, they were free from its social obligations and political maneuverings. Their only interest seemed to be what was best for Islam and for Egypt. The altruism of the new rulers and the economic strength of the sultanate brought years of stability and prosperity to Egypt under Mamluk rule. However, the Mamluks continued to shun any attempt to integrate into Arab society.

The Decline of the Mamluks' Power

The fall of the Mamluks was linked to a disaster Europe was also to undergo: bubonic plague. "The Black Death" began to spread in the middle of the 14th century. It reached the Levant through Christian merchants and mariners. The impact was devastating. In a matter of years, hundreds of thousands died and entire villages became ghost towns. People scrambled to find uncontaminated drinking water – many fled to neighboring countries, literally running for their lives. Almost no one was left to farm the land, and trade slowed to a trickle.

Because the situation was the same all over Europe, no European enemy could exploit the empire's weakness, but the chaos and the instability attracted the attention of the Bedouins, people not much in contact with society and therefore not affected by the plague. Bedouin raids became common. They came to pillage and plunder, increasing the insecurity and chaos that already prevailed. The authorities could hardly retaliate; the Black Death had decimated the army, the fortresses had been abandoned, and the highways were virtually unprotected.

The plague sapped the empire's strength and its treasury, and Mamluk influence began to wane. It ebbed severely after the onset of the plague because the subject Arabs had tolerated their rule only so long as the Mamluks provided security and prosperity. When Western Europe found a way to avoid the empire and still trade in the Far East, it was a severe blow.

For centuries, all European goods transported overland were forced to traverse the Mamluk Empire en route to the Far East, and all trade caravans were taxed as they traveled through. This had long been a thorn in the side of the Christian countries, because any increase in the Mamluk treasury was used in part to maintain its troops; thus Western Europe found itself, in the pursuit of trade, helplessly contributing to the upkeep of an enemy army.

Constant attempts were made by Christian countries to find a different route to the Far East. Both land and sea routes were investigated. The journey of Christopher Columbus was the most famous of several attempts.

As we know, Columbus did not find India as he had hoped to, but his voyage encouraged others. It was the Portuguese Vasco De Gama who in 1497 circumnavigated Africa and sailed on to India. Once the sea route was proven, Western Europe had access to Egypt through the "back door:" the Red Sea.

This was deeply disturbing to the Mamluk Empire. If European fleets were to act cooperatively in the Mediterranean and Red Seas, the empire could fall. On top of that, any European fleet that sailed up the Red Sea could endanger the Muslim holy

holy sites in Mecca and Medina. Hastily, the Mamluks began to erect numerous fortresses on the eastern shores of Egypt. To add to their concerns, news came of the Ottoman conquest of Byzantium.

The Ottoman Attack

On the northern borders of the Mamluk Empire, a small kingdom of Turks led by the House of Othman was gaining power. Having survived the last brutal attack of the Mongol Tamerlane, they had recovered quickly and headed west to capture Constantinople, the capital of the Byzantine Empire. When the plague loosened the Mamluk grip on its own empire, the Ottomans were poised to take hold.

Along with these worries an event had taken place that would change the world forever but would uniquely impact the Mamluk Empire: the invention of gunpowder. The Mamluk pride of conquest was based on courage, and each warrior's ability to demonstrate his skills in hand-to-hand combat on the battlefield. As weapons using gunpowder were developed, the skill and courage of the Mamluk warriors became useless – an enemy could kill them from yards away. Yet the Mamluks themselves refused to take up these new weapons. Perhaps this refusal, more than any thing else, brought down the Mamluk Empire.

In 1516, after having defeated the Persian army and secured his eastern border, the Ottoman sultan Selim was ready for war. He led his army into Syria – Mamluk territory – and attacked. While the Egyptian army raced to the rescue north across Israel, the Mamluks tried to negotiate a treaty but Selim refused. On August 24, 1516 near Aleppo, the Mamluk army was defeated. The way was clear – the Ottoman army could storm into Egypt.

As the Turks marched south through Israel, the cities fell one by one.

The Mamluks had finally purchased cannons and rifles and a few scattered shards of the Mamluk army tried to keep the Ottomans from reaching Egypt until fresh forces could be amassed for defense, but it was too late. In January 1517, what was left of the Egyptian Mamluk Empire ceased to exist.

The Mamluk Legacy in Israel

During the two and a half centuries of Mamluk domination in Israel, the land witnessed the construction of a significant number of Muslim religious institutions, the road system was vastly improved, and for a long time the country enjoyed relative stability and prosperity. Politically and strategically however, Israel was in continuous decline. Its governors under the Mamluks were generally men of low status who had been sent to Israel as punishment. A position in Israel was in effect an exile from the political centers and therefore from political power. Jerusalem was regarded as a religious center only and the walls of the city had been left in ruins. The road into the city was also neglected and in bad condition.

In contrast, the main highways were well kept: army posts, inns and way stations were spaced along the main road – primarily a postal road to speed information and intelligence (from Israel and Damascus) to the Mamluk government in Cairo.

While the coastal cities had been leveled and the harbors filled in with rubble, much construction had taken place inland, especially along the roads. The Mamluk sultans gave their attention mainly to religious buildings. The fact that they did not begin their lives as Muslims produced an obsession to prove their loyalty to Islam – and the best way to do so was to dedicate huge chunks of the treasury to the Muslim clergy, as well as the construction of Madrassas (religious schools) and mosques.

The religious building projects were especially beneficial to Jerusalem. Haram A-Sharif (the Temple Mount) received special attention, and many inns and pilgrim hostels were built in the city. Every sultan, every governor, every high official in the Mamluk administration would add something to the Haram and to Jerusalem. The city's water system was repaired and the market places were rebuilt.

The most significant change in Israel during the days of the Mamluk Empire was the shift in its demography. The Mamluk Empire had absorbed many refugees fleeing from the Mongols, and settled them in Israel. Most of these were Muslims of non-Arab descent: Kurds, clans from the Caucasus Mountains, Turkish tribes, and more.

Israel had been only a minor province in the Mamluk Empire. When some of the displaced Turkish nationals (having fled their own lands to escape the Mongols) asked the Mamluks for asylum, they were offered land in Israel. Those settlers added yet another piece to the ethnic puzzle that had come to represent the land of Israel.

Very few Christians had stayed in the land. After the long struggle between Muslims and Christians in the years of the Latin Kingdom, the Muslim tolerance was close to zero. Only some clergy from Eastern origins remained in Israel and the Franciscans, who were active in guarding the holy places – despite the fact that many were in ruins.

Although Christian inhabitants were few, many Christian pilgrims continued to visit Israel, and the Mamluk government could not ignore the financial benefits of such visits. To guarantee that pilgrims continued to come and spend their money, special arrangements were made by the authorities to ensure their safety. State officials escorted the pilgrims' caravans and the price for such services was fixed by the state. During the fourteenth and fifteenth centuries, hundreds of thousands of Jewish and Christian pilgrims came; the Mamluk era saw pilgrimage to Israel reach its peak.

While Muslim religious zeal for Israel and especially Jerusalem was increasing, the authorities also gave rights to Jews and Christians. In some cases the Muslim clergy criticized these actions, but the Mamluk authorities put internal stability and prosperity even before religion.

Most of the Christians came only for pilgrimage. In the case of the Jews, however, many came to stay. The pressure on the Jews in Christian countries had continued to grow, reaching its climax when the inquisition in Spain and Portugal targeted them as Christianity's main enemies. When given the choice to convert or be deported from their homelands, many chose to leave.

The only destinations where they might expect tolerance were Muslim countries. The Muslim authorities saw no threat in Jewish merchants and artisans settling in Jerusalem – Jews had no disagreements with Muslims over holy sites, and the two religions could more easily co-exist. In addition, the Jews had seen the collapse of the Byzantine Empire as a divine sign that the Messiah was coming; and many Jews returned to Israel in anticipation of that event.

With the Christians however, there were conflicts over a wide range of issues. The local Muslim communities lacked the resources of the Europeans; the money Christians sent to redeem holy sites spotlighted the inequality and created tension between the two groups.

The Mamluk authorities, torn between the obligation to support the Muslim cause and the need to maintain reasonable relationship with Christian countries, trod thin ice. They were resented by fellow Muslims and by the subject Christians.

By the time the Ottomans had replaced the Mamluks in Israel, all who lived in the land spoke Arabic. In many ways, although there were several ethnic groups, all with different customs, everyone was part of the Arab culture.

16

The Ottoman Era
c. 1516-1917

North of Palestine in Anatolia (an area representing modern-day Turkey), The House of Osman had clawed its way from mediocrity among numerous Turkish clans and gained incredible power. As the Ottoman Empire, it would dominate the Middle East and influence the entire world for centuries.

The early Ottoman beys (clan leaders) first annexed large parts of Anatolia, taken from weaker clans. Ottoman power grew far beyond Anatolia in the 16th century under the leadership of Selim I: he conquered the Mamluks and claimed their substantial territories. Under his son, Suleiman, the Ottoman Empire expanded even further. It grew from about two and a half million square miles to over sixteen million before it disappeared in the twentieth century.

Since the Ottomans were Muslim, their annexation of the Holy Land probably seemed to many to be no more than the exchange of one Muslim overlord for another; but unlike previous conquerors, the Ottoman Empire had staying power. It was able to maintain its hold in the Levant and North Africa well into the twentieth century. From the heady days of "Suleiman the Magnificent" to the dog days of "The Sick Man of Europe," the Ottoman influence made its mark on Israel, sweeping in like a rising tide, tossing her roughly about, and eventually depositing her on the shores of the modern era.

The Ottomans were a society doggedly isolated from the West. During the time European society was birthing epic events that would echo down through the centuries, Islam incubated slowly, stubbornly. Israel and the rest of the Ottoman Empire ignored the Renaissance, the French Revolution, and the Industrial Revolution: since Islam was the ultimate way of life, what could be learned from the Europeans?

The new Ottoman masters were not Arabs, but as devoted Sunni Muslims they considered it their responsibility to maintain the Muslim holy sites in Israel as well as to provide safe passage for Muslim pilgrims. Despite its religious significance, the region was of little importance to the empire. The Sultans in Istanbul (the former Constantinople) appointed its governors (either locals employed by the Ottomans or officials sent over from Turkey), but otherwise left Israel mostly alone.

In some areas the Ottomans appointed local lords, who were often given the title "Pasha," which originally was a military title but came to refer to any high-ranking Turkish official. As long as the lords could maintain law and order and send their taxes in on time, Ottoman interference was infrequent and benign. Some of these local lords accumulated so much power that their domains became semi-independent.

One of these lords, the Mamluk El Gasali, had been appointed as governor of both Syria and Israel by Selim I, soon after the Mamluks were defeated. Once in office, El Gasali fired the Ottoman-appointed officials and installed his own appointees. When news reached him of Selim's death in October 1519, he had become so powerful that he dared to declare himself Sultan. He was killed in 1521 – powerful, yes, but not more so than the Ottomans.

The Druze Fakhr A-Din

Another example of a powerful subject lord was the Druze Fakhr A-Din. In the mountains of Lebanon (Druze territory) the locals had been given partial autonomy, and whenever the central authorities were too weak to exercise control over a certain area, it became an open invitation for the local lords to increase their own influence.

During such an opportune time, Fakhr al-Din was able to extend his authority far beyond what had been approved by Istanbul. He was able to do so by first gaining a reputation among the Ottomans as a competent ruler, leading the Ottoman authorities to place more and more provinces officially under his control. Encroaching then on other territories, the Druze leader eventually oversaw a large area that included most of Israel.

Attempting to further strengthen his own position, A-Din independently established diplomatic ties with the Vatican and the European principality of Tuscany. The Vatican was pleased to support his military efforts against the Ottomans in return for the promise of control of Jerusalem and its holy sites.

Due to his alliance with the Vatican, Fakhar al-Din openly supported the Christians and gave Christian communities in his territory the right to restore churches and monasteries that had lain in ruins since the Muslim conquest. That was too much for the current Ottoman Sultan: in fear for his life, Fakhar A Din had to flee to Europe.

He returned five years later in 1618, his ambitions still high. He built fortifications, allegedly to stabilize a line against the Bedouins (who continued to raid the empire's borders), but actually to prepare for war against the Sultan. He attempted to conquer Jerusalem, but was unsuccessful.

For nearly forty-five years, from 1590-1634, Fakhar A-Din made his presence known. He was deeply involved in commerce with European countries. Under his leadership, new markets were opened up for olive oil and cotton. The local cattle were improved through the introduction of European stock. Roads were paved, bridges fixed, and the harbors of Beirut and Acre were renovated.

His successes and his alliances with Christian countries led to his downfall, however. The Sultan was uneasy with A-Din's growing independence and western friendships. An Ottoman fleet was dispatched from Turkey while an Ottoman army marched from Damascus, intent upon neutralizing the Druze. Fakhar A-Din eventually turned himself in and was executed in Istanbul in 1635.

Daher El-Omar

The ruling Sultan was also forced to yield occasionally to the demands of local sheiks in the effort to keep Ottoman territories stable under the yoke. In fact, the sultans often approved powerful sheiks as legitimate rulers of their districts. One of the strongest Bedouin lines, by then well established in Galilee, was the El-Omar family. Its youngest son, Daher, was made the ruler of the district of Tiberias.

Daher's idea of inter-territorial diplomacy mirrored that of a gangster: He harassed Damascus by repeatedly robbing the native population. (Banditry was definitely illegal, but such localized problems did not garner much attention in Istanbul as long as they did not affect the Ottoman treasury.) The governor of Damascus did not retaliate, fearful that the rulers in Istanbul would consider his action overly aggressive. It was not until Daher made an actual attempt to conquer Damascus that Istanbul issued a decree permitting the Pasha of Damascus to pursue Daher and destroy his power base.

Well prepared, Daher withdrew to Tiberias and took shelter behind the same massive walls he had ordered built years before. For several months in 1742, the fortress survived repeated attacks. Large caliber cannons were brought from Turkey by sea, to shell the city's walls while a regiment of diggers tunneled under them. For two weeks, Ottoman artillery launched hundreds of cannonballs with no success. While waiting for reinforcements, the Pasha of Damascus died, and the Ottoman army eventually left Tiberias without dealing with Daher.

Daher's next step was to offer to purchase from the Pasha of Sidon (where Tiberias was located) the right to collect taxes. This request was approved, and with it came official recognition from Istanbul of Daher's new position as Pasha of Galilee.

Within a few years, his domain covered most of Israel and part of the mountains of Lebanon. As his power grew, the possible threat it represented to the Sultanate did not go unnoticed. Although Daher had promised to pay the Sultan's debts and had received an official title in return, the Sultan determined to get rid of the rebel. A large army and a large fleet were sent to Israel. Daher's capital city of Acre, on the Mediterranean Sea, was bombarded. He was shot as he fled the city with his family, and died on August 22, 1775.

For forty years Daher controlled the area with little opposition, but his sons, ruling after him, constantly warred with each other, leading to the dissolution of the house of Daher in only a few short years.

Jazzar and Napoleon

Ahmed al-Jazzar (Daher's long-time opponent) was soon appointed governor of Acre. He immediately had to deal with the Bedouins; Daher had been of Bedouin descent and some of these tribes were still loyal to his memory. Upon Daher's death, they had rebelled and spread their own kind of chaos. They repeatedly attacked and plundered rural areas and occasionally even cities. Finally, after great effort and with the empire's assistance, the Bedouins were driven out, although it wasn't until 1781 that Galilee finally came under Ottoman sovereignty once again.

Jazzar had a private army of fifteen thousand men, sustained by his own treasury. They were loyal to him, since he and not the empire paid their wages. Jazzar, who was of Bosnian descent, had been educated in Egypt on Mamluk principles, which made him a talented soldier and commander. None of this made him popular in the Ottoman court, but he proved to be a very efficient ruler in the service of the Ottoman Empire, and is credited with reestablishing Istanbul's power in Galilee and other areas of Israel.

Commerce flourished under Jazzar. Most of the trade came through merchants from France, who had established themselves in Acre and some of the harbor cities along the Lebanese coast. Jazzar encouraged the economic growth, but he also inflicted heavy taxes on foreign trade, reducing the French profit. France, therefore, preferred a governor more congenial toward French interests.

In May of 1789, a mutiny broke out in Jazzar's army. He was able to suppress the coup, but expelled the French consul to Joppa because the French had supported the rebel leader. Several weeks later, Jazzar deported all French merchants from Acre and Beirut, confiscating their possessions and their property. When the French complained to Istanbul, an imperial decree (a Firman) was issued, ordering Jazzar to allow the deportees to return, and to compensate them for their loss of property and other damages. Jazzar ignored the decree.

In 1797, a French army officer came to Acre and confronted Jazzar regarding his refusal to return French property and reinstate France's right to trade. Jazzar refused to negotiate with him but permitted some French merchants to reside in Acre. The fact that Jazzar, an Ottoman subject, refused to submit to an imperial decree, and that the French delegate spoke directly to a local ruler (rather than with the administration in Istanbul) shows the growing weakness of the Ottoman government. The empire that a century before had terrorized Europe, threatening the gates of Vienna, was in rapid decline.

The tremendous changes taking place in Europe were hardly felt in Israel, although they had some effect on the border provinces – Russia had been recognized as custodian of the Greek Orthodox Church after it defeated the Ottoman Empire in 1774, and European countries had been granted trade rights. Those trade rights translated to political power and influence in the provinces when each European power would bribe Ottoman officials to gain the Sultan's ear.

As long ago as 1535, an agreement had been signed between Suleiman the Magnificent and the King of France, which granted France preferred trade status with the Ottoman Empire, and recognized France as the protector of Catholic interests in the Ottoman territory of the Levant. In short, France was considered the close friend of the Ottoman Empire.

It came as a surprise, therefore, when a French army commanded by Napoleon landed in Egypt in 1798. However, Napoleon had not come to avenge Jazzar's treatment of French merchants. His objective was to cut off the land route between Britain and its richest colony, India. Napoleon had corresponded with Jazzar in Acre instead of consulting the government in Istanbul, which was caught by surprise and certain that Britain would retaliate if Napoleon were allowed to pursue his objective.

In desperation, The Ottoman authorities formally sanctioned Jazzar's growing power by appointing him governor of Syria and Egypt. He was ordered to stand against Napoleon. With the empire officially behind him, Jazzar began plans to defend Acre and the rest of Israel.

A large number of troops were sent to Gaza. The British navy offered massive assistance. Jazzar commanded the land effort and the Ottoman navy was to attack by sea. While the Ottomans were still preparing, Napoleon decided to strike.

His army crossed the Sinai and after only a few days stood at the gates of El Arish, on the edge of Israel. What was left of his fleet sailed to Acre carrying large-caliber cannon. The British navy was able to seize the French artillery, but Napoleon's ground operation conquered Gaza, Joppa and Haifa. By March 19 of 1799, the French army was encamped around the walls of Acre.

Napoleon planned to subdue Acre and to use its massive fortifications to stand against the approaching British and Ottoman armies. For two months, his efforts were fruitless as Jazzar's men successfully defended the city. Seeking to take advantage of Napoleon's preoccupation there, a large Ottoman army assembled near Damascus and marched toward Acre. On April 6, although severely outnumbered, the French army defeated the Ottomans; the French general's goal seemed within reach.

A British-Ottoman army was making its way to Egypt to cut off the French forces. While still far distant from the enemy, it received unexpected assistance that ensured victory: a plague decimated the French army, killing many soldiers and weakening those who survived. Napoleon was compelled to evacuate Israel in June of 1799, leaving behind some of his troops and much of his armament.

Napoleon's invasion, the most significant event of Jazzar's reign, signaled the growth of European involvement in the Ottoman Empire and especially in Israel.

By the time of Jazzar's death in May of 1804, he had brought Israel from years of chaos into a season of relative prosperity and stability. Jazzar in some ways duplicated the pattern set by Daher El Omar: a local ruler who theoretically was subservient to Istanbul but retained great personal power.

Jazzar, like other powerful Pashas, were appreciated by the Ottoman Empire when trouble threatened; but all too often such men were assassinated after their immediate usefulness waned – the empire did not want to promote their power. Perhaps, had the empire rewarded such men instead of killing them, it might have been less vulnerable to both foreign threat and domestic turmoil, neither of which were never far away.

Muhammad Ali

All too soon after repelling Napoleon, Ottoman rule was challenged again. This time the threat came from the subject overseer of Egypt, Muhammad Ali. An Ottoman army officer of Albanian descent, Ali had been appointed governor of Egypt in 1805. A man of many talents, he was dedicated in his desire to develop Egypt: experts from Europe were employed to improve agriculture and industry. The Egyptian army was restructured, based on the European example.

As a loyal Ottoman subject, he was called upon to suppress a revolt in Hijaz (the Eastern shores of the Red Sea, modern day Saudi-Arabia) and to assist the Ottoman army in its efforts to quell Greek national ambitions. In order to do so, he was forced to put a significant strain on Egypt's economy. As compensation for this, and as a means of replenishing Egypt's treasury, he demanded that the Sultan place Syria and Israel under his sovereignty.

The Sultan of course refused. Muhammad Ali then sent his son Ibrahim to Israel with ten thousand infantry, two thousand horsemen, and eight thousand camels carrying supplies. Crossing the mountains of Judea and Samaria and traveling along the shores of the Mediterranean Sea, Ibrahim reached Acre with minimal resistance. He prepared for a long siege.

Ibrahim's first attempt to take the city was made on March 3, 1832. Acre was spared, thanks to its skilled commander. As Ibrahim prepared for another attack, his intelligence sources informed him that Ottoman troops were advancing rapidly through Syria. He left Acre and marched north to confront the Ottomans. In the battle, in April of that year, Egypt decimated the Ottoman army, crushing Acre's hope for rescue. Ibrahim returned to Acre and a month later, on May 27, beset from land and sea, the city surrendered to the Egyptian army. The Egyptians then quickly overran Syria, which offered but weak resistance.

Encouraged by that success, Muhammad Ali then sent the Egyptian army deep into Ottoman territory. In Konya, only about two hundred miles from Istanbul, the Ottoman army was defeated. As result of this victory on December 21, 1832 (despite massive European pressure that forced Ali's army to withdraw), Ali now ruled over an area larger than all the territories of the Ottoman Empire.

The Egyptians fortified Acre, and began to institute new standards. Much of the populace chafed under the new regime, especially the Bedouin tribes. They were used to lawlessness, possible through the timely bribes of Ottoman rulers. The Egyptian officials were not so easily persuaded. When Ali decided to draft the peasants and Bedouins into the Egyptian army, the area erupted in violence.

Former local officials who had lost their positions joined the Bedouins and farmers in open revolt. On May 14, 1834, a force of thirty thousand rebels penetrated Jerusalem through a forgotten sewage canal and captured the city. Ibrahim and his troops arrived at Jerusalem two weeks later, and on May 31, in a battle that ranged as far as the outskirts of Bethlehem, the rebel forces were scattered.

On June 4, another large force gathered in Bethlehem: the Bedouin tribesmen of Mount Hebron had come to avenge the defeat of their colleagues. The revolt was suppressed in a confrontation near Solomon's Pool south of town, and completely crushed in a battle near Hebron in July of that same year.

After Ibrahim had demolished the Ottoman army and successfully besieged Acre, the Ottoman Empire sought help in their conflict with Egypt. Concerned about the worsening situation and Russia's growing appetite for Ottoman territory, the Europeans came to the rescue and a British-Austrian fleet laid siege to Acre.

On November 3, 1840, during a bombardment, a shell hit the city's arsenal and detonated thousands of tons of explosives and ammunition. This was the first time in history that the new explosive aerodynamic shell had been used. The huge explosion killed some seventeen hundred people and the walls of the city were breached as well.

In the chaos that followed, an elite Austrian force, arriving by sea, entered Acre and captured its citadel. At dawn, when the Egyptian defenders saw the Austrian banner waving from its peak, the army ceded the city and began its withdrawal to Egypt. Muhammad Ali's short reign over Israel and Syria was over: the Europeans had returned Israel to the Ottoman Empire.

Despite its brevity, Ali's reign over Israel had been eventful. His attempt to change the pattern of government to a European model modernized the country. The Egyptians also abolished hundreds of years of Muslim superiority by requiring them to pay taxes like any other inhabitants of the land. The laws that had prohibited non-Muslims from riding horses and waving Muslim banners were rescinded. Christians and Jews had been invited to live in the land and were given permission to erect new churches and synagogues.

Although the value of Israel as a land bridge to the Far East had been recognized for some time, the Egyptian threat had brought it to the forefront of British and French attention. Both powers preferred a weak Ottoman presence in the area rather than control by the stronger Egyptians. The first European consulate (that of Great Britain) opened in Jerusalem in 1838, foreshadowing an intensified European presence in Israel, and broadcasting Europe's growing desire to gain a foothold in the area.

One of the ways for Europeans to increase their influence in Israel was by protecting the holy places and the local Christian groups. France had been recognized as a patron of Catholic interests. Russia had become the official protector of Greek Orthodox concerns, and the minority Protestants and Jews were protected by Great Britain.

This was in many ways a reflection of Europe alliances, with a coalition between Britain and France on one side against Russia on the other. But the debate surrounding the holy sites was not the only controversy: the Europeans living in Israel were personally protected by their patron countries, resulting in small autonomous groups that enjoyed rights and protection the locals did not have.

In fact, the special privileges given to Christians caused great discontent among the local Muslims; the country found itself in the midst of turmoil over issues that had nothing to do with domestic matters. The escalating involvement of Europeans in Israel was one of the catalysts for yet another war over the area (the Crimean War, from 1854-1856), although the conflict took place outside Israel's borders.

The Ottoman Empire, now drained of resources and bankrupt, had turned again to Europe for financial assistance and manpower in order to attack Russia. They received assistance from those European powers that had a vested interest in halting Russia's expansion. The thousands of British and French soldiers who took part in the Crimean War were in fact protecting Europe itself from Russian encroachment.

The Bosporus, also known as the Istanbul Strait, separated European Turkey from Asian Turkey. "The sick man on the Bosporus," holding the front line against Russian expansion, was indeed close to death. Only European intervention prevented disaster. It was yet another example of the Ottoman Empire's increasing dependence on Europe.

International Attention

The growing British interest in the area – primarily to protect the land route to India – eventually translated into aggression. In 1869, the Suez Canal (a man-made canal that allowed shipping between Europe and Asia without circumnavigating Africa) was in operation. In 1875, Britain acquired majority control of the Suez Canal by purchasing forty-four percent of its shares. In 1878, Britain took Cyprus, which had been under Ottoman control and was key to the canal's protection. In 1882, the British army invaded Egypt (essentially occupying it, although officially it remained Ottoman territory). In Istanbul, Britain began to be viewed as an enemy. When, with the protection of the canal in mind, Britain tried to redraw the Ottoman borders and push the Ottoman forces as far away as possible, all semblance of friendliness vanished.

After long debate and sporadic armed conflict, an agreement was signed on October 1, 1906, between Great Britain and the Ottoman Empire, fixing the border between the two in a line connecting Rafah (on the shores of the Mediterranean Sea) with Taba, on the Gulf of Aqaba. This border has served the Sinai ever since, and today stands as the international border between Egypt and Israel.

The Ottoman Empire was trudging towards it end. Over several decades it had appeared obvious that Britain was turning away from any previously stated desire to preserve the Ottoman Empire. This caused the Ottomans to search for an alternative, and they found an ally in Germany.

Most of Germany's military attention had been focused in central Europe. Under the leadership of Otto von Bismarck, Germany had no strategic interests in any political or religious issues in Ottoman territory. Unofficially however, the situation was different: German members of a christian sect called the Templars were building colonies in Israel and thousands of them resided in the land.

The growing Teutonic interest in Israel resulted in a long list of distinguished guests: The Austro-Hungarian Emperor Franz Joseph and other European notables crossed the land on camels' humps, pitching their tents under ancient olive groves on the terraced hills of Judea and Galilee.

In 1898, the German emperor Wilhelm 2nd visited Israel. The royal yacht docked at Haifa, at the edge of the German colony. While there, Wilhelm gave much of his attention to the German settlers. Although the Templars was not supported by the state, its members represented significant German involvement in Israel simply by virtue of their large numbers. Well prepared to accommodate a multitude of German pilgrims, they were an inviting presence to their countrymen.

By the end of the nineteenth century, Germany was the most influential foreign group in Israel, but other countries were also making their presence known. The British had founded the Palestine Exploration Fund (PEF) to survey the land and learn more about its past. From across the Atlantic Ocean, Americans began to visit, and many became interested in founding colonies in Joppa and Jerusalem. Virtually ignored during centuries of Muslim domination, Israel had finally caught the attention of individuals as well as of nations.

The twentieth century brought a change in the standard of living. European architecture began to crop up in the newer sections of Jerusalem as well as in other places. Christian interests had covered the country with a network of roads and railroads. German settlers brought modern machinery; Jewish settlers brought water pumps and introduced new methods of agriculture.

The Zionist movement, which had been founded in 1897, had initiated large-scale land purchases, and farming communities were established in several areas. As new settlers bought land and played a part in the economy, Israel entered an era of prosperity. In 1904, after a pogrom (a more or less government-sanctioned campaign of persecution) in Kishinau, Russia, about thirty thousand Russian Jews fled to Israel – adding significantly to the number of Jews already living there.

There was, however, a major difference in the Christian and the Jewish objectives in coming to Israel: the Christian interests were dedicated to gaining access to Christian holy sites in order for Christian pilgrims to visit them and worship. The Jews, on the other hand, came with a national vision: to see the Jewish people restored to their ancestral homeland, and to become a nation once again.

The Ottomans were unhappy to note the growing power of Christians in Israel, but the growing influence of the Jews created other headaches. The Arab-Muslim inhabitants of Israel became increasingly dissatisfied with the changing complexion of the land, and local Arabs exerted pressure on the Ottoman government to put a halt to the purchase of land by Jews.

Israel was changing so rapidly it is hard to say what happened first. Christian pilgrims became a common occurrence in Israel: hundreds of thousands of Russian pilgrims overflowed the harbor of Joppa, the streets of Jerusalem, and the banks of the Jordan. Russia's Tsar Nicolas I saw to the construction of facilities to house them.

Western pilgrims, wealthy and used to comfort, demanded better facilities and services. New hospitals provided modern medical care. This was attractive to the Christian Arabs, and the Greek Orthodox Church (with which many Christian Arabs in Israel had been affiliated) began to cede its superiority to the Catholic and Protestant churches.

The penetration of Europeans and Americans into Israel had begun from strictly a religious perspective, but this was soon followed by economic investment and before long, it involved political power: first the clergy, then the business interests, and finally, the consulates. The armies were yet to come. The arrival of every additional priest, merchant, and diplomat pried loose the Ottoman grip.

In tandem with the weakening of the Ottoman Empire, Israel's own strength was growing, as these other nations established interests in the land and then protected them. The country was to some extent a reflection of the complicated situation in Europe: the rivalries playing themselves out on the world's stage were taking place in Israel as well.

Once World War I commenced (and the Ottoman Empire allied with Germany) the Ottoman authorities introduced a harsh policy against all foreigners in Israel. The local Arab population was recruited into the army and to auxiliary brigades. Jews who were Ottoman subjects were drafted and sent to the Caucasus Mountains, while foreigners were expelled from their homes and accused of collaborating with the British army. Residents in the land who refused to accept Ottoman citizenship were expelled, some fifteen thousand by the end of 1915.

Communication with the outside world virtually stopped and domestic industry came to a screeching halt. Many of the Jewish ultra-Orthodox communities had existed solely through donations from Europe and the United States; that money was suddenly no longer available; the financial aid that had streamed in from around the world had dried up. Some seventy thousand Ottoman troops spread throughout Israel, chopping down trees, confiscating livestock, and raiding crops. In some places people were exiled from their homes, only to find when seeking shelter elsewhere that other communities had also been devastated.

The Balfour Declaration

While the inhabitants of the land suffered under the horrors of war and the destruction it brought, British and French politicians were drawing maps to mark the division of the Ottoman Empire at war's end.

On November 2, 1917, the Balfour Declaration was published. It was made public before the British were officially in control of Israel, but the eventual outcome of the war was already evident. The Declaration announced for the first time the right of Jews to a national home in Israel. On December 11, 1917, the Ottoman Empire surrendered Jerusalem to the 60th Infantry Division of the British army, and over twelve hundred years of virtually continuous Muslim rule (interrupted only briefly by the Crusaders) came to an end.

The British commander General Edmund Allenby entered Jerusalem on foot, saying that no Christian should enter in an arrogant way the city where Jesus had suffered. The conquest of Jerusalem by the British army was splendid news to Christians around the world: the bells of Westminster Abbey rang for the first time in three years. In Rome, all the church bells pealed for a complete hour. Special prayers were offered in the Cathedral of Notre Dame in Paris.

Allenby, when he took command over British forces in the Middle East, had promised to hand over Jerusalem as a Christmas present to the British people that year. He kept his promise.

The British offensive had pushed the Ottoman troops north to the mountains of Samaria and onto the plains of Jezreel. That historic battlefield, the scene of countless conflicts since Biblical days, became the stage for yet another historic clash, the battle that would push the Ottomans and their German allies out of Israel.

The final blow came between September 19th and 25th: the Ottoman army was destroyed in a week. At the end of September in 1918, the fighting moved to the eastern side of the Jordan River, and Israel's future passed into British hands.

17

The British Mandate 1918-1948

The League of Nations formalized Britain's oversight of Israel in 1919, but the British Mandate over Palestine was actually the result of agreements and decisions that had been made about Israel long before the Ottoman Empire was defeated and World War I was over.

Previously, in 1916, Britain and France had entered into a secret understanding concerning each nation's sphere of influence in the Middle East. According to this agreement (called the Sykes-Picot Agreement after the men who negotiated it), most of Israel was supposed to be an international zone. However, by the end of World War I the British army was firmly entrenched in Israel, and the League of Nations therefore gave Britain alone a mandate over the land. The mandate spoke succinctly of the British obligation to assist the Jews in developing the land and preparing for Jewish independence.

A homeland for the local Arabs was not discussed, but in reaction to the mention of a Jewish homeland, the Palestinian Arabs also demanded immediate recognition as a nation. In an attempt to forestall violence, the British created the "Supreme Muslim Council" in response to Arab demands. It was in charge of Muslim affairs, but its main focus was religious. This did not satisfy the Arab nobility, who wanted much more. (The Syrian city of Damascus had actually been conquered and occupied by the British, who had turned it over to the Arabs under the leadership of Prince Faisal. The Sykes-Picot agreement, however, had promised Syria to France, and when the French army ultimately took over Damascus and expelled Faisal, the Arabs felt betrayed by the British.)

The growing tension produced wave after wave of riots, beginning in April of 1920. The Jewish community in Jerusalem was attacked by an Arab-instigated mob. The Haganah (a Jewish paramilitary organization organized to guard Jewish farms and settlements) was formed at about this time in response to the belief that the British did not intend to protect Jewish citizens from Arab attack.

In 1921, in retaliation for Faisal's expulsion from Damascus, Jews in Joppa were attacked and more than forty were murdered. When the Arabs and Bedouins went on to attack British army bases, British retaliation was severe: hundreds of Arab militiamen were killed and the leaders were expelled from the country, A form of peace prevailed, but the Middle East was far from stable. Over the next thirty years, Israel's history would be polarized around Arab-Israeli strife and ineffectual British attempts to defuse it.

On June 3, 1922, a statement of policy – what the British called a "White Paper" – was issued. The area across the River Jordan was given to Abdullah, the brother of Faisal, and Faisal himself was appointed as king of Iraq – a country founded especially for him. The British hoped that by these moves, the civil unrest and dissatisfaction would disappear. They did not.

During the 1920's, the population of Israel grew enormously. The British turned all of their attention toward stemming the tide of illegal immigrants who were arriving by sea, while the inland borders went unguarded. Thus, hundreds of thousands of Arabs from other parts of the Middle East were able to enter Israel illegally. In contrast, the British Navy carefully vetted the European Jews attempting entry from the coast. Israel began to fill up with Arabs.

Because of the animosity between Jew and Arab, any overt support of Jewish Nationalism by Britain created a political minefield. The Arabs had supported Great Britain during World War I, and the British could not dismiss the fact that their former ally might be needed again. The British desire to please the Arabs often came at the expense of the Jews. Every few years a new policy was announced. In examining these statements, one can detect a gradual withdrawal by the British Empire from the obligations it had previously espoused regarding Israel.

Interestingly enough, such announcements always came after the Arabs had initiated a wave of unrest in Israel. The riots of 1929, ostensibly a dispute regarding the Wailing Wall, caused the death of more than one hundred and thirty Jews; yet the British refused to interfere. The result of the riots was another "White Paper," calling for Jewish land purchase to be forbidden, in response to Arab concerns. That the land in question was mostly the property of Arab landlords happy to sell appeared not to factor in the decision.

Adolph Hitler had been made Chancellor of Germany in early 1933. In response, a flood of Jews chose to leave Germany, and many of them immigrated to Israel. Up to that time, most of Israel's Jews had come from Eastern European countries. In general, German Jews were of a higher economic status and their arrival gave a significant boost to the economy. New industries, construction, and increased farm production were seen throughout Jewish areas, and cultural life flourished as musicians and other artists settled in Israel.

Arab dissatisfaction over this influx of Jews was the main reason for the Arab Revolt in April of 1936. British officials at first excused the revolt as the outcome of legitimate Arab concern over the growing Jewish population and purchase of Arab-owned land. When the revolt degenerated into a gang war – thousands of Arabs killing other Arabs and Arab gangs repeatedly attacking British troops – Britain finally retaliated. Troops were sent from other parts of the British Empire to maintain law and order in Israel. While the British were still preparing for a counterattack, they recruited to their assistance the only loyal group in the region – the Jews. A Jewish militia was formed, which joined the British forces patrolling the border. In a short time, a fence was built along the borders between Israel, Syria, and Lebanon.

During the time the inland borders had been more loosely guarded, thousands of Arab gang members had entered Israel clandestinely. When the Arab revolt intensified, Britain launched an attack aimed at flushing those Arabs from their hiding places: rural villages and secret bases. British military attacks on the villages caused great loss of life and severe economic damage.

The situation in Israel was growing more problematic by the minute. In London, it was understood that such military actions had to be carried out jointly with political initiatives if the problems in Israel were ever going to be resolved. Accordingly, a royal commission was formed, headed by Lord William Robert Peel.

Peel was not part of the British administration, and was therefore free to make non-partisan observations. Spending two month in Israel, he met with delegates from all sides and published his report in July of 1937.

Peel's report did not favor Great Britain – the British authorities, wrote Peel, had violated the original meaning of the Mandate by failing to assist the Jews in forming their own homeland. He criticized the British for allowing thousands of Arabs to enter Israel by crossing its interior borders unchallenged. However, recognizing that the Arabs were already a significant and probably immovable presence in the land, he recommended that Israel be partitioned into two independent states – Jewish and Arab.

It was the first official mention of partitioning. Both parties rejected the proposal, and the violence – subdued for a time – erupted once again.

With the devastation of the Arab economy and the expulsion of the most militant anti-British Arab leaders, it seemed as if Britain was siding with the Jews. As long as Britain held out the possibility of a Jewish state, it would be considered an Arab enemy, something to be avoided as the world headed toward war. To minimize the damage done to the Arab cause and to retain their support, Britain had to officially distance itself from any alliance with the Jews.

The public change in British policy was announced in another White Paper, penned by the British Colonial Secretary Malcolm McDonald; it amounted to an open repudiation of the Balfour Declaration.

McDonald's White Paper, dated May 17, 1939, called for a limit on Jewish land purchase as well as restrictions on Jewish immigration. It declared openly that the Balfour Declaration had been a mistake. The new British policy stated that within ten years, an independent state would be established in Israel based on its present demography – this meant a country that would be two-thirds Arab, not an independent Jewish State. The Jewish population was shocked by Britain's decision: it now seemed obvious that Britain did not intend to keep its promises to the Jews or to give up control of the region.

Between 1936 and 1939, more than sixty Jewish communities had been founded. Jewish society had become better organized and had developed a form of government that was surprisingly able to create unity among the different ethnic Jewish populations. All in all, the Jews had tried to work within the confines of the Mandate but were no closer to their dream of a re-established homeland than when the Mandate had first been announced. Ultimately, Jewish leaders felt that the only possible response to the new declaration was armed struggle. The Haganah began to use its British-learned skills against British military targets in Israel. (At this point, the Jews and the Arabs were not yet in continual conflict with each other. The initial struggle had been between the British and the Arabs – this next between the British and the Jews.)

On September 1, 1939, World War II erupted and the situation in Israel changed. The British had to let go of their hope to draw the Arabs to their side when Mufti (a title for an expert on Muslim law) Haj Amin al-Husseini, from his shelter in Berlin, declared that all Arabs should fight with Nazi Germany. After all, said the Mufti, the Germans have our same objective – to destroy the Jews.

Disappointed – and perhaps desperate – the British asked the Jewish authorities to encourage their men to volunteer for the British army. Some forty thousand Jews from Israel volunteered to serve the British Empire, although their main motivation was probably not the preservation of the British Empire but the defeat of the Nazis.

During five long years of war, the British showed zero tolerance for political unrest and Israel remained relatively tranquil, but Jewish patriots were not inactive. Jewish soldiers in the British army were gaining valuable combat experience; Jewish leadership was fighting for permission to bring ships full of European Jews home (past the British blockade of Israel's coast).

On May 8, 1945, Germany surrendered and the war in Europe ended. Only then was the horror fully unmasked: about six million European Jews had been brutally exterminated: men, women, and children.

The Holocaust engendered broad sympathy for the Jewish cause, and international attention focused on Israel. Jewish organizations worldwide persisted in their efforts to halt the British immigration blockade, still in place after the war. Under American pressure, Britain finally issued one hundred thousand immigration permits to Jewish refugees.

The conflict between the Jews and Britain, mutually abandoned during the years of World War II, now resurfaced. The Jewish underground, composed of three groups, initiated numerous operations against the British army all over Israel. Most of the time the three groups acted separately.

When British intelligence arrested and later executed members of the underground, British soldiers were kidnapped and hanged in retaliation. On July 22, 1946, the three Jewish underground groups joined forces and blew up British headquarters in the King David Hotel in Jerusalem. The British responded not by targeting the underground, but by arresting and exiling many of the Jewish leaders in the forefront of the civil struggle.

While the situation in Israel intensified, Hagganah operatives traveled throughout Europe, purchasing ships and gathering Jewish refugees to bring them to the homeland. The whole world despised the British for sending their sleek battleships against the old boats full of traumatized Holocaust survivors, whom they refused to allow on Israeli soil. In most cases the refugees were sent to concentration camps in Cyprus; sometimes they were ordered back to Europe. Widespread public opinion criticized Britain's anti-Jewish policy in Israel.

On February 15, 1947, the British Prime Minister Ernest Bevin stated that Great Britain would leave the future of Palestine in the hands of the United Nations. The British hoped that the U.N. would reaffirm the original mandate, wherein the U.N. had pledged non-involvement in Israel. This would give Britain the freedom to treat the situation in its own way.

The U.N.'s response was to send a committee to Israel. For five weeks during June and July in 1947, the committee members researched the situation, holding meetings with Jewish leaders. The Arabs boycotted the meetings and refused to send representatives to present their case. In August the United Nations committee published its report.

The U.N. committee recommended partition of the land: sixty-two percent Jewish, thirty-eight percent Arab. According to the recommendation, Jerusalem would stay in the hands of an international tribunal. Due to pressure put on the United States by Britain, the land ratio was eventually dropped to 55/45, still favoring the Jews. The Arabs continued to reject any solution save for a completely Arab state in Palestine. On November 29, 1947, the issue was brought in front of the U.N. general assembly. Thirty-three nations were in favor of the plan, thirteen were against, and there were ten abstentions.

The Partition Plan, now known as Resolution 181, had determined several things:

1. The British Mandate in Palestine would terminate no later then August 1, 1948.
2. Two states would be established, based on the partition suggested: a Jewish state and an Arab state.

3. An international tribunal would be in charge of Jerusalem.
4. A U.N. committee of five members would assume power from Britain and transfer it to the new Israeli and Arab governments.

With the political climate in the Middle East and the refusal of the Palestinian Arabs to accept the partition plan, war in Israel was inevitable. Inflammatory statements were delivered by Arab politicians from surrounding countries, stating that the Arab regular armies would never accept a Jewish state in their midst. The message came across loud and clear: if the Jews dared to claim their homeland, the Arab armies would "throw the Jews into the ocean."

All parties began to prepare for Israel post-mandate. However, with the British presence in Israel still over ninety thousand strong, the changes came slowly.

The hostilities commenced on November 30th' 1947, one day after Resolution 181 was made public. Arab gang members attacked a Jewish bus on its way to Jerusalem and six of its passengers were killed.

18

The State of Israel 1948

Volunteers from Arab countries were storming into Israel to assist their Arab brothers. Busy with their own evacuation, the British ignored most of the activity. The Arab attacks grew bolder as the end of the mandate drew near.

In the first part of what is known in Israel as "The War of Independence" the Jews were strictly on the defensive. Jordanian troops (commanded by British officers) were fighting alongside the Palestinians fully armed – with British approval – but the British restrictions on firearms had kept the Jewish troops from being adequately supplied.

Jerusalem and the roads leading to it were the focal point of the initial conflict. Since the road to the city traveled through a narrow mountain path (The Gate of the Valley), Arab villagers on both sides of it were blocking passage and firing on Jewish vehicles. This narrow gorge, flanked by steep hills, was a battlefield for several weeks: vital supplies were prevented from reaching Jerusalem.

As things worsened in the city, and food and water became dangerously scarce, the Jewish leadership changed its strategy of retaliation only and went on the offensive. In an effort to lift the blockade, they decided to attack the Arab villages along the Gate of the Valley.

This proved to be a turning point in the first stages of the war. After successfully breaking the blockade and ensuring a continuing supply of food and water to Jerusalem, the Jews launched attacks on additional Palestinian areas. In most cases they succeeded: Galilee, the coastal plains, and Haifa came into Jewish hands. Hundreds of thousands of Palestinian Arabs fled as a result.

Although the Jews expelled some Arabs from their homes – mostly along the Jerusalem corridor to lessen the chance of future supply blockades – most Palestinian Arabs abandoning the area did so after nearby Arab nations offered to shelter them during what was expected to be a short-term conflict. Caravans of Arab refugees filled the roads as they traveled towards the Jordan River, north into Lebanon, and into the area of Gaza. The Jews had won the war within Palestine, but now Arab armies waited just outside Israel's borders, ready to invade the new Jewish state as the clock ticked down on the British Mandate.

In contrast to its thirty years of life, the mandate expired quietly. On the morning of May 14, 1948, the last British flag was slowly lowered from its mast in the port city of Haifa. Sir Allan Cunningham, the last British High Commissioner of Palestine, saluted, boarded his flagship, and sailed for home. British control was over and both Jew and Arab prepared for the next round: the Jews determined to establish their nation, and the Arabs determined to prevent it.

Independence and War

At 4:00 pm on Friday, May 14, 1948, David Ben Gurion, the head of the Israeli provisional government, read the proclamation of independence from Tel Aviv. A bitter argument had preceded this event: several believed that the new nation's ability to survive an

Arab attack was very low; they feared total annihilation once the declaration was made. The day was getting older and the Sabbath commenced at sundown; unless the vote was finalized quickly, it would have to be postponed. Hastily, the document was signed. However, it was not until Sunday, when the Sabbath was over, that the pronouncement was broadcast: the establishment of the State of Israel.

Thousands, hundreds of thousands, gathered in the streets, pressing in close to scattered radios and loudspeakers, to hear the glorious words spoken. Solemn, attentive quiet gave way to riotous cheers as Jewish men, women and children danced in the streets, tears coursing down many faces.

As the new nation of Israel opened her arms to the world, Europe's Holocaust survivors flooded in, sometimes going directly from ship to battlefield. Other volunteers, mostly Jews, came from everywhere, some of them veterans of the recent war.

The Arab response to Jewish independence was immediate – armies flooded in, intent upon making good the Arab threat to "throw the Jew into the ocean." Every man and every rifle were vital for the protection of the new nation. Weapons, purchased earlier from all across Europe in the anticipation of need, were now shipped to Israel.

The ongoing war and the logistical burden of assimilating the immigrants proved to be a drain on the young country's resources. There were also other challenges: The provisional government had to move quickly to integrate the three former underground organizations into a single army under its control. This was accomplished only after a conflict that almost led to civil war; but the growing external pressure on the new state compelled the rivals to put aside their differences and stand together.

On June 11, 1948, a short ceasefire was declared. The Jordanian army had failed to conquer Jerusalem, but the line separating the two armies put the old city of Jerusalem (including the Jewish quarter) in Jordanian hands. The larger portion, however, belonged to Israel. The new State of Israel had not only survived the consolidated Arab aggression, but in some places had enlarged its territory.

Israel appreciated the intermission. During the lull, money, weapons, and manpower arrived in large numbers, shifting the balance of power in favor of Israel. The war continued until the beginning of 1949. The Arab armies were not only expelled from Israel's territory but Israeli forces had also penetrated deep into parts of the Sinai – Egyptian territory.

An Uneasy Peace

Israel was in prime position to negotiate, and official talks were held on the Isle of Rhodes. One by one, the Arab countries signed a ceasefire agreement with Israel. The first agreement was forged with Egypt: Israel vacated the Sinai including the Gaza Strip. Next, Israel agreed with Lebanon to pull back to the international border established by France and Britain after World War I.

An agreement with Syria was forged slowly; Syria was the only country involved which currently occupied land that had been given to the Jews during the partition. Negotiations ended on July 20, 1949, with a full Syrian withdrawal from the areas west of the Jordan, and a rather more vague consensus on several issues concerning the eastern side of the Sea of Galilee. Iraq, which had pulled its forces out in March of 1949, did not take part in the negotiations, having refused to be involved in any talks with Israel.

Israel had felt that Jordan was the one country with which a genuine peace could be achieved. However, the assassination of

Abdullah, the King of Jordan, on July 20, 1951, ended the talks and also the chance for peace between the two countries.

For the first time since the division of the kingdom after Solomon's death, the land of Israel (the area between the Jordan River and the Mediterranean Sea), was divided among three national entities: Israel, Jordan and Egypt; but none of them were completely satisfied with their portion. Palestinian refugees still crossed the unprotected borders bent on revenge, expressing their frustration by killing Jewish settlers and damaging farm equipment.

In the first decade after independence, the young state concentrated its energies toward accommodating Jewish refugees from Europe, North Africa, and Asia. The new nation was covered with transit camps built to shelter the immigrants who continued to pour in. In fact, Israel's Jewish population would double in the first three years. Providing housing and jobs and integrating the refugees into the economy challenged the new government. An economic crisis and other pressing needs resulted in food rationing for several years. Finally, with financial aid from Jews around the world, the government stabilized the sagging economy.

The new Israeli government was also engaged in a never-ending struggle against terrorism, initiated and financed by Arab supporters in Egypt and Jordan. The Palestinian Arabs who had fled Israel into these countries at the onset of the war had expected their stays would be temporary. Instead, they were now stranded, subsisting on government aid. The host countries exploited these often poor and mostly homeless refugees, training many of them and sending them back into Israel on missions of destruction.

The committees that had been formed to ensure the implementation of the ceasefire agreements were not effective.

The agreements were based on the assumption that the parties would work together and make progress toward a lasting peace, but those issues that had not been specifically addressed during the cease - fire talks could not now be resolved. Arab and Jew would simply not agree.

Despite such setbacks, some vital projects were completed in the years after the ceasefire. The most important of these was the draining of the Hulah swamp in northern Israel. Under constant Syrian fire and Israeli counter-fire, the work was completed in 1957. The drained swamp yielded highly fertile acreage, significantly adding to Israel's agricultural capacity. The endeavor also ensured increased Israeli settlement near the Syrian border.

Just a few years after the War of Independence, the nation became divided over Germany's offer of payment to Israel as compensation for the millions of dollars worth of property taken from Jews during World War II. Many Israelis were victims of German atrocities and survivors of the Holocaust, and only seven years had passed since the end of the war. The wounds were still raw, and the acceptance of what many called "blood money" was unthinkable. Demonstrations and riots broke out in front of the Parliament building while it debated the issue.

Eventually, pragmatism prevailed: Israel needed the money. Despite the emotionality of the issue, the agreement was signed on September 10, 1952, between Conrad Adenauer, the German Prime Minister, and Moshe Sharet, Israel's Foreign minister. Israel would receive economic compensation for the brutalities of the Holocaust.

The Arab countries around Israel kept talking about the "second round" that would defeat the Jewish state. They were taking steps to accomplish their goal. Both the Egyptian and Jordanian armies were openly involved in military operations against Israel. Israeli retaliation did not achieve peace, and tensions continued to mount.

In July of 1956, Gamal Abd El Nasser, the president of Egypt, announced the nationalization of the Suez Canal. The traffic through the canal, up until then operated by Britain and France, had been protected by international convention and was open to free shipping. Nasser's announcement changed all that. Now the jurisdiction, revenues, and administration of the canal would be under Egyptian control. Nasser's announcement created an international crisis, especially for France and Britain.

Egypt's Nasser had already established a reputation as a pan-Arabic leader, because of his aggressive stance toward western attempts to maintain colonial interests in Egypt. When he had announced (in September of 1955) that Czechoslovakia had agreed to supply weapons and other military surplus to Egypt, western nations realized that Arab militancy in the Middle East was an ongoing threat: the appropriation of the Suez Canal was only the beginning.

As this event unfolded, the Egyptian army was at the same time engaged in a military action against Israel, blockading its southern shore. The announcement about the Suez Canal pinpointed the world's eyes and ears on the Middle East – and brought Israel's situation to worldwide attention.

For some time, Israel had been seeking its own munitions supplier, and had been refused by both the United States and Britain (each refused to sell arms to any Middle Eastern country). When Egypt nationalized the Suez Canal, the nation of France soon agreed to supply Israel with arms. The French government had come to the realization that a well-armed Egypt might easily overcome its neighbors, severely reducing any chance to regain control of the canal. Finally, powerful western nations were partnering with Israel to the same end: to sap the growing strength of Egypt and prevent it from becoming a superpower in the region.

In an attempt to regain jurisdiction of the canal, Israel, France and Britain joined together. A ground operation was to be conducted by Israel and followed up by the arrival of British and French forces by sea and by air at Port Said, the northern entrance to the canal.

On October 29, 1956, the Israeli army crossed the border into the Sinai Peninsula. Three days later, the Israelis halted ten miles east of the Suez Canal, after devastating the Egyptian army. The arriving British and French troops were supposed to clear a strip ten miles long on the western edge of the canal and secure it from both sides; but the operation was delayed, and as a result of heavy pressure from the United States, was never even carried out.

In March of 1957, Israel pulled out of the Sinai. The operation had achieved its goals: the blockade on Israel's southern shores was lifted, international traffic through the Suez Canal was resumed, and the attacks on Israel from Egyptian territory ceased.

Domestic Challenges

By the end of this first decade, Israel's population was 1.8 million, three times more than in 1948. While the first ten years had been dedicated to simply absorbing the flood of immigrants and protecting Israel borders, now the focus was shifting toward the social challenges facing the new society.

The immigrants had come mostly from North Africa and Asia. Their living conditions in Israel were generally poor, as the majority of them arrived in Israel without property and with minimal education. There was a huge, frustrating chasm between their standard of living and those of other social groups. They were also the objects of discrimination. Despite a sincere attempt to address these issues and improve the circumstances of the immigrants, the solutions were only partially effective and the inability to implement lasting change would lead to further discontent and widespread riots in the future.

Although Israel had just won the war with Egypt, little changed between Israel and her Middle East neighbors. Whenever they sensed weakness and found opportunity, they did not hesitate to attack. Israel sought to deter her Arab adversaries by the purchase of a powerful advantage: a nuclear reactor was obtained from the United States in May of 1959. Soon after that, France supplied another reactor. In order to make these purchases, Israel had to state officially that the new facilities would be used only for civil projects.

By the end of the 1950's the Jewish state still had no constitution. Without one, some of the most fundamental issues that underpin a nation cannot be codified, and Israel faced such an issue: the name "Jew" in modern times wears two faces: it has a religious as well as a national definition.

According to the "Law of Return," immigrants arriving in Israel had to prove that they were Jewish. The rabbinical identification of a Jew differed from the state definition used to establish citizenship. The attempt to create a Jewish homeland was challenged throughout by the various opinions of what that homeland ought to be. Many Jews were no longer religious. They maintained their culture, and even the form of their religion – but their Judaism was, by their own admission, purely ethnic. They had no desire for a religious government.

The debate continued to rage as to how to synchronize the two identities of the Jew, especially as to defining which aspect ought to have the superior claim. Until this could be done, the constitution would have to wait.

The 1960's

On April 11, 1961, the trial of Adolph Eichmann, a Nazi war criminal, opened in Jerusalem. Eichmann had been captured several months earlier in Argentina, where he had resided since fleeing Germany in the late 1940's. He was an important Nazi official, and had ordered the torture and death of countless Jews and other ethnic minorities.

The trial was a chance for the Israeli public to face the horrors of the Holocaust. For years, most survivors had preferred to hide their stories, through misplaced guilt and shame. Native-born Israelis could not understand how the European Jews could have so easily submitted to the appalling brutality. Holocaust victims were often accused of cowardice. Survivors learned to keep quiet.

The trial lifted the veil from the horror, and uncovered the methodical and deceivingly benign campaign the German government had waged against the Jews. Most had chosen early on to "wait out" the situation, for persecution and prejudice were familiar trappings to the Jew. By the time the deathly consequences of Hitler's "Final Solution" were obvious, it was too late for them to leave – too late to save themselves. And those who might have made a difference – their gentile neighbors – had been brainwashed and intimidated by the Third Reich. There was no one to turn to and nothing to be done.

The evil exposed by the trial caused many of those who had previously shunned the survivors to embrace and support them instead. The disclosures of the trial, as painful as they were for so many citizens, offered an opportunity for national healing from the events of World War II. Eichmann was found guilty and was executed on May 31, 1962.

At Israel's northern border, Syria continued its assaults. For a number of years, Israel had been working on a system to bring water to the Negev Desert from the Sea of Galilee. When the system was officially opened on June 10, 1964, the Syrians (who also claimed the Sea of Galilee as a water source) intensified their attacks against Israel.

Also In 1964, the Arab League founded the Palestinian Liberation Organization. Its original charter stressed the right of return for Palestinian Arabs as well as the annihilation of the State of Israel. Even though the PLO eventually became the official representative of Palestinian interests and joined Israel around the negotiation table, for the first several decades after its inception its main business seemed to be to fund acts of terrorism against Israel. (Yasser Arafat was its chairman from 1969 until his death in 2004.)

In 1966, the military rule that had been imposed on Israeli Arabs since the establishment of Israel was terminated. While they possessed the right to vote, few Arabs were active in Israel's political or public life. The Israeli government invested in Arab villages and towns, seeking to improve living standards and offer opportunities for Arabs to integrate into the national mainstream. To some extent these efforts, while a step in the right direction, were "too little, too late." Arab-Israeli history had never been amiable; there was little chance it could ever be.

As it had been from the first day of Israel's existence as a nation, the fight for survival was not over. The unrest along the northern border, the Arab leaders shouting about a "third round," these and other things led to another armed conflict – the Six Day War.

For the past several years, Arab countries had been equipping themselves with Soviet weapons and ammunition. Russia had also extended diplomatic support, sending advisors to both Egypt and Syria. The Soviet presence in the Arab Middle East can be attributed to its desire to undermine American economic and strategic interests there – especially regarding oil. Russian propaganda portrayed America as a dangerous pro-Israeli power, an enemy of all Arabs.

Incendiary speeches by Arab leaders encouraged frequent demonstrations in the streets of Cairo, Damascus, and Amman, demanding the eradication of the Jewish state. By May of 1967, Egypt was prepared to attempt it, and Egyptian forces began streaming into the demilitarized Sinai Peninsula. The U.N. peacekeeping forces, stationed in the region since the Israeli withdrawal in 1957, were ordered by President Nasser to leave.

Three days later, on May 18, the U.N. soldiers vacated the Sinai, leaving the Egyptian and Israeli armies facing each other at Israel's southern border. On May 23, Egypt blocked the Straits of Tiran, Israel's gateway to the Indian Ocean, Africa, and Asia. To the north, the Syrian army prepared to join the conflict. (In November of 1966 Egypt and Syria had signed a treaty of mutual assistance in case of war with Israel.) When Jordan announced it would also participate in an assault on Israel, the seriousness of the situation was magnified. Israel stood alone, without any military or diplomatic support.

Egypt's president Nasser declared: "We intend to open a general assault against Israel. This will be a total war. Our basic aim will be to destroy Israel." (May 26, 1967.)

Israel decided not to wait for Egypt's offensive and launched its own. On June 5, 1967, the Israeli Air Force struck the Egyptian

Air Force and destroyed more than three hundred airplanes on the ground. In destroying Egypt's planes, Israel gained complete control of the airspace above the battle zone. When Jordan began shelling West Jerusalem, The Israeli Air Force responded quickly. Syrian targets to the north were also destroyed.

This incredible six-day war, Israel's greatest and most decisive military victory, brought amazing results. Arab armies were devastated; Israel's new boundaries tripled its territory and cushioned Israeli settlements against Arab weapons launched from the new borders. Jerusalem, a divided city for nineteen years, was – geographically at least – made whole again after a short and fierce battle on June 7, 1967.

Israel's new boundaries followed the topography: the River Jordan to the east and the Suez Canal to the south. North, next to Syria, a range of extinct volcanoes and Mount Hermon were incorporated into the Israeli border.

The end of 1967 marked the beginning of Israel's third decade of independence. The Arab countries (Jordan in particular) were sheltering Palestinians who continued to mount an armed struggle against Israel. The Israeli-Palestinian conflict had replaced the Israeli-Arab one.

For three years along the southern border, Egypt and Israel pounded away at each other, as a war of attrition raged. Heavy exchanges of fire caused hundreds of casualties for Israel and thousands for Egypt. A new fighter jet, the F-4 (supplied to Israel by the United States), had changed the balance of power along the Israeli-Egyptian front: the new aircraft's capabilities allowed Israel to mount air attacks deep into Egyptian territory. Egypt and Israel were both ready for a ceasefire.

Large construction projects had been initiated in East Jerusalem, the Golan Heights, and a few locations in Judea. However, the Israeli government still held the opinion that peace with its neighbors could be achieved through the exchange of land. Therefore, authorization for settlement and construction in the disputed territories was given only to a small degree.

The 1970's

In 1971 Israel's population passed the three million mark as heavy immigration continued. Even though Israel was enjoying its recent military victory and new international reputation, many Israelis were restless and unsatisfied: North African and Asian immigrants regarded as a betrayal the state's inability to integrate them socially. They were disappointed with the lack of resources available to them as well. Many took part in riots and demonstrations to express their discontent.

Their struggles caught the attention and support of social activists, and the news coverage of riots and other signs of dissatisfaction gave the impression of a national crisis. While the situation was not as grave as portrayed by the media, the problems could not be solved quickly and would continue to simmer.

The focus on social affairs lasted but a short time, however, and was soon replaced by a more pressing and sadly familiar issue – terrorism had begun to haunt the nation. Israel found itself the target of an intense effort to demoralize and terrorize its citizens through sporadic but deadly aggression: Israeli embassies, airports, and other sites were attacked. On May 30, 1972, twenty-five people were killed in the Tel Aviv airport by Japanese terrorists. On September 5, 1972 during the Munich Olympics, Palestinian Liberation Organization (PLO) terrorists murdered eleven Israeli athletes.

On Israel's borders, the Egyptians and the Syrians were poised to attack. Ever since the humiliation of the Six Day War, they had looked forward to revenge. Anwar Sadat, the current Egyptian president, had previously proposed a land exchange in return for peace. Golda Meir's government had declined the offer. Sadat then stated he was willing to sacrifice a million soldiers to liberate Arab occupied territory. Both Egypt and Syria began to prepare their forces. Arab arsenals overflowed with Soviet-supplied munitions, weaponry that boasted the best of available technology.

Unaware that the Arabs possessed new anti-aircraft missiles and anti-tank rockets (along with an unabated determination to destroy their Jewish neighbor), Israel was extremely vulnerable. However, flush from its recent military successes and occupied with domestic matters and terrorism, Israel believed that the likelihood of Arab attack was small.

On October 6, 1973, when millions in Israel were observing the high holy day of Yom Kippur (the Day of Atonement), the Egyptian army advanced across the Suez Canal and initiated what came to be known as The Yom Kippur War. At the same time, north along the Golan Heights, columns of Syrian tanks crossed Israeli anti-tank canals and penetrated Israeli lines on their way to the Jordan Valley and the Sea of Galilee. Caught in a vise between two enemies, Israel faced its greatest military challenge.

Eighteen days of war followed, days in which the Israeli forces were able to strike back effectively at Syria being halted only as they drew near Damascus. In the south the Egyptian advance had been brought to a standstill when Israeli troops crossed the Suez Canal. Israel surrounded the 3rd Egyptian Army and captured the area on both sides of the canal. There were hardly any Egyptian forces left to prevent a deadly advance on Cairo, and a negotiated ceasefire went into effect on October 24, with Israeli soldiers camped a mere sixty-five miles from the Egyptian capital.

The war, although a military victory, caused a political earthquake in Israel. Army intelligence had failed to identify the Arab weapon systems that had caused hundreds of Israeli casualties; the government had not recognized the need of or called for national preparedness. Soldiers returning from the battlefield felt betrayed. Some were trapped in their bunkers for days along the Suez Canal, cut off from the rest of the army, and no one had come to their rescue. Israeli arsenals, instead of being well equipped and organized, had been in far from satisfactory condition.

Demonstrators outside the Parliament building in Jerusalem, and in other places all over the country, demanded an inquiry. The pressure on the government was intense. On November 18, 1973, a national committee was appointed to investigate. The committee published a partial report on April 1, 1974. Placing the blame on the military, it held that the Chief of the General Staff was accountable for the lack of readiness and for the failure to mobilize the reserve forces prior to the assault; the Head of Military Intelligence and the Chief of Southern Command were accused of the same charges. The government itself was cleared from any wrongdoing.

The Israeli public exploded, incensed that the government refused to accept any responsibility for the nation's blindness leading up to the war. While the Six Day War had represented the apex of the Israeli army's achievements, the Yom Kippur War instituted a national demand for accountability in government.

Weeks of demonstrations followed. Golda Meir was forced to resign. The new Prime Minister was Yitzhak Rabin, the hero of the Six Day War. The Labor Party remained in the majority, but national opinion continued to shift. (In the next general election in May 1977, a discontented electorate would shun the Labor Party, virtually erasing the power it had held since Israel became a nation.)

The Yom Kippur War delayed some of the intended social and religious reforms, but did not forestall them completely. The territories continued to be the main concern. Gush Emunin, a religious national group, was founded. Its platform was built on the belief that Jews had the right to live anywhere in Israel, and that in fact living in Judea, Samaria, the Gaza Strip, or the Golan Heights was a religious commandment. Of course they did not neglect to also point out the strategic value of establishing Jewish settlements in the heart of Arab-populated areas. Even as the government discouraged settlement in the territories in anticipation of future land concessions to Arab nations, once Israelis had settled there, resources became available to fortify the territories and benefit their inhabitants.

On June 26, 1976, Palestinian terrorists hijacked an Air France jet traveling from Paris to Tel Aviv. On board were 83 Israelis and other passengers. The plane was forced to fly to Uganda, a country that had expressed support for the Palestinian cause. The terrorists demanded that their comrades (imprisoned in Israel and elsewhere) be released.

The Israeli government declined to negotiate, instead employing military tactics to free the hostages. On July 4, 1976, Israeli Special Forces landed in the Ugandan airport at Entebbe, where the hostages were being held. The Israeli soldiers killed the terrorists and freed the hostages, displaying Israel's determination not to concede to terrorism.

In some ways, life went on as usual, but beneath a surface contentment, political and social dissatisfaction continued to grow. The Labor Party, held by many to be responsible for the catastrophe of the war in 1973, became mired in financial scandals. Party and state officials were prosecuted for misbehavior and corruption.

The Likud Party, led by Menachem Begin, was the Labor Party's main opposition. As evidence of misconduct within the Labor Party mounted, the Likud Party gained popularity. During the campaign leading up to the 1977 elections, Begin centered his platform on social issues. While a brilliant speaker, he was in essence a simple man. His personality appealed to many people who had become apathetic toward the present government. Israel was ready for a change.

In the May 1977 elections, The Labor Party lost its majority, and for the first time since its independence, the State of Israel had a new leading party. The incoming conservative government instituted a major change in the Israeli approach to the territories: instead of a wait-and-see attitude, large-scale settlement was encouraged.

The economy was also addressed: the exiting government had invested heavily in domestic finances, essentially dominating Israel's business and industry. In October, The new government announced that it would not continue the practice. The public was invited to participate in the new tax-free stock market. It was hoped that this would increase the flow of currency and jump-start the sluggish economy.

While the new government was still feeling its way, an unexpected proposal came from Egypt: President Anwar Sadat stated that he was willing to come to Israel and address the Israeli Parliament (the Knesset) in order to open peace negotiations. The following day, Israel extended a formal invitation. On November 19, 1977, an Egyptian airplane touched down on the runway of the Tel Aviv airport. President Sadat and his entourage stepped out onto the tarmac, and his historic trip to Israel commenced. During his three-day visit, the Egyptian president addressed the Knesset. In his speech, he pressed Israel to evacuate of Sinai Peninsula and find a solution to the Palestinian problem. It went unnoticed at the time, but the peace process for the Middle East started.

Sadat's visit to Israel created a breach in the Arab world, however: it was seen as a traitorous threat to Arab solidarity. As a result, the PLO intensified its attacks on Israel's northern border, even as Israel and her southern neighbor (Egypt) began to move toward a negotiated peace.

On March 11, 1978, eleven PLO terrorists landed on the shores of northern Israel, traveling by speedboat from Lebanon. Their mission was to take as many Israeli hostages as possible and to free Palestinian prisoners in Israel. They commandeered a bus full of passengers and made their way towards Tel Aviv.

That Saturday afternoon the roads were crowded. The terrorists cut a bloody path, shooting at cars and throwing hand grenades. The bus was stopped at a police checkpoint outside Tel Aviv. In the battle that followed, nine terrorists were killed. Unfortunately, thirty-five passengers also died, some by friendly fire. It was another example of Israel's determination to deal harshly with terrorists – even if civilians were also destined to pay a price.

Several days later, Israeli forces invaded south Lebanon, seeking to destroy the Palestinian "state within a state" which existed there. This Israeli action created a crisis in the Israeli-Egyptian peace talks then taking place. The talks were delayed until after the Israeli troops pulled out of Lebanon.

On March 26, 1979, in the United States capital of Washington D.C., the Israeli-Egyptian peace accord was signed. Israel promised to pull out of the Sinai within three years (1982), and the two countries agreed to maintain open borders. Each nation promised to establish embassies in the other country and encourage reciprocal commerce and tourism.

A by-product of the Israeli-Egyptian talks involved the territories: Israel agreed to give full autonomy to the Palestinians in Judea, Samaria, and the Gaza Strip. In 1978 when the offer had first been tendered (and turned down by the Palestinian leadership), only five thousand Jews had resided in these areas. Subsequently, Jewish settlement had been encouraged, and dozens of Jewish communities were now established in these territories. This would lead to unhappiness and loss later on as concessions were made in pursuit of peace.

The 1980's

Because the leaders of Israel were forced to stay constantly watchful amid the bubbling caldron of the Middle East, they were often compelled to make rapid decisions when trouble threatened. In 1981, Iraq's nuclear reactor (supplied by France) was in a very advanced stage of operation. Although Iraq's president, Sadam Hussein, had stated frequently that Israel was not the main target of Iraq's nuclear weapons, Israel did not trust these statements. On Sunday, June 7, 1981, Israel launched a pre-emptive strike against the facility. Israeli fighter jets leveled the reactor to the ground, removing that nuclear threat from Israel for decades.

That same year on December 14, Israel officially annexed the Golan Heights. Unlike most of the other territories, there was general agreement as to the strategic value of the territory, since Syria had shown no signs of joining the peace process. By law, all the inhabitants of the Golan, Jews as well the local Druze, became citizens of the State of Israel.

While many issues regarding the territories were still subject to debate, this did not hinder settlement activity, and even though Israel teetered on the edge of financial catastrophe, the amount of money invested in the territories continued to grow, despite the fact that inflation was sky-high. It appeared the conservative government's privatization of the country's assets had failed to stabilize the economy; the consequences of too-rapid expansion and bad financial management would eventually boomerang against the Prime Minister.

In spite of all the other problems, the Israeli-Egyptian peace agreement was moving forward; as per the agreement, Israel had vacated most of the Sinai, and it was now time to implement the last part of the treaty – the complete evacuation of any Israeli settlements still there. Some five thousand Israelis were living in the Sinai at this time and were determined not to leave their homes without a struggle. Hundreds of soldiers and policemen were employed in the evacuation efforts – which ended with the Israeli communities razed to the ground.

The harsh removal of Jewish settlers from the Sinai ripped at the conscience of the nation. While a vast majority in Israel favored the Israeli-Egypt agreement and understood that the evacuation had to take place, the images of fellow Jews being torn from their homes against their will were burned deeply into Israel's collective memory.

Meanwhile, on Israel's northern border, the PLO was getting stronger, demonstrating its confidence by firing hundreds of rockets into Israel. On June 6, 1982, Israel invaded Lebanon once again.

While the previous assault on Lebanon in 1978 had been limited, this operation, Peace for Galilee, had far-reaching goals: destroying the PLO only in south Lebanon had not proven sufficient. The new plan was to arrest or deport from Lebanon all those engaged in acts of terror.

Despite being warned not to fire on Israel's forces or actively support the PLO, the Syrian regime ordered its troops deployed in Lebanon since 1976, to shoot at the advancing Israeli soldiers. Nevertheless, by the second week of the war, Israeli forces had surrounded most of Beirut (the Lebanese capital), and the important Beirut-Damascus highway was under Israeli control.

For several weeks, West Beirut (the location of PLO headquarters) was the focal point of the fighting. Israel refused to allow the deployment of a U.N. force into the area until the PLO had removed its forces from Lebanon. During the conflict, an American negotiator of Lebanese origin, Philip Habib, crossed back and forth between the two parties, trying to arrange an evacuation of Palestinian forces from Beirut and end the war.

On August 21, the first group of PLO members left the city, followed by more than ten thousand other terrorists and Syrian soldiers. However, many PLO members remained in Beirut in violation of the agreement, and when opportunities arose, hostilities were resumed.

Part of Israel's aim in its action against Lebanon had been to affect the political situation in Lebanon in favor of the country's Christians, who were Israel's allies. In Lebanese elections during the war, Bashir Jumail, the head of the Christian Phalanges (Lebanese Christian paramilitary groups), had been elected president on August 23, 1982. Jumail was supposed to take office a month later, but on September 14, a bomb exploded at Phalange headquarters, killed him and some of his men.

A wave of outrage swept through the Christian Phalanges. Representatives of the groups asked Israel to give them access into two Palestinian refugee camps in Beirut, claiming that Jumail's assassins were hiding there. Israel granted the request. On the night of September 16, 1982, members of the Phalanges massacred hundreds of Palestinian men, women, and children in the Sabra and Shatila refugee camps. Israel was vilified internationally for allowing this entrance into the camps.

As the military action in Lebanon strayed further from its stated objectives, the Israeli public grew restless, questioning the war itself and the role of Israeli officials in the massacres at the refugee camps. In demonstrations in Israel, Secretary of Defense Ariel Sharon was called on to take responsibility and to resign his post. A committee of inquiry eventually declared Sharon responsible for having allowed the Phalanges to enter the camps (albeit with no awareness of their intention). Sharon was forced to resign his office; however, he remained a cabinet member. (The Israeli presence in Lebanon lasted eighteen years. Eventually, Israel pulled out from the Beirut area and formed a line further south.)

In January of 1983, the Israeli stock exchange collapsed. The political, military and economic situations finally overpowered the Prime Minister, Menachem Begin, and he resigned on August 28, 1983. The next election was a surprise – a virtual draw between the two major parties. An emergency government was formed, and the two parties shared the position of Prime Minister on a rotating basis every two years. The elections had signaled the need for change, but neither party held the perfect answer. Social ills and terrorism had not been eradicated, and the economy was still in crisis. By January of 1985, the inflation rate in Israel had risen to four hundred percent.

Despite these trying circumstances and the ongoing challenges of integrating new immigrants into the society, Jews of every nationality were always welcome to return to their homeland. The Aliyah, or ascent, is the Hebrew term given to the immigration of Jews into Israel. In countries where such immigration is forbidden, the Mossad (Israel's intelligence agency) operates clandestinely to accomplish Aliyah. For instance, between the end of 1984 and the first few weeks of 1985, intelligence agents escorted seven thousand Ethiopian Jews into the country via the Sudan. A change in Ethiopia's regime had put these Jews in danger; with a few well-placed bribes, the Mossad was able to bring them safely into Israel.

The nation continued to navigate its way through the rough seas of political turmoil within and the rocky shores of terror and violence without. Security needs were enormous, the economy still struggled, and social tensions continued to mount: Jews and Arabs, secular and religious, rich and poor, left and right, each segment had its own agendas and opinions.

The administration of the territories continued to be a divisive issue. Improvements there were often at the expense of needs in other areas of the country. The towns in Galilee and in the Negev were neglected in many ways but those in the territories enjoyed a wide range of benefits: housing was cheap, roads were paved, and high-level services were widely available.

However, the Palestinians living in the territories were unhappy with their low standard of living and their low status: they grew increasingly restless. In December 1987, while Israel's attention was focused on the economy and social issues, the volatile situation erupted. It began in Gaza and spread to other Palestinian cities, towns, and villages. The Israeli army was somewhat bewildered as it confronted not soldiers, but children – children throwing rocks and Molotov cocktails.

This political unrest, named The Intifadah (Arabic for "shaking off" and the common Arabic term for an uprising) provided the perfect opportunity for various Palestinian militias and rival gangs to fight one another. Palestinian gangs killed more fellow Palestinians during the uprising than did the Israelis. Palestinian citizens were accused by other Arabs of cooperating with Israel and were executed without legal proceedings. The infighting was widespread, but the Palestinians had little unity of purpose. The

Intifadah dragged on for over two years but accomplished little for the Palestinian cause.

The PLO had finally been expelled from the area and new local leaders had emerged: in 1988, a new Palestinian religious movement, Hamas, was founded. Supported by Iran and Syria (which where both anti-PLO), Hamas was built on a religious zeal that refused to recognize or negotiate with Israel; this laid the foundation for ongoing conflict.

The 1990's

When the Soviet Union collapsed in 1991, it opened the immigration gates of Russia, the Ukraine, and other former Soviet republics. Many Russian Jews took this opportunity to flee to Israel.

The events in the former Soviet Union had come as a total surprise to most of the world, and Israel was severely tested as it attempted to absorb over two hundred thousand immigrants in just one year. Providing housing, jobs, healthcare and other basic services proved immensely challenging. In the midst of these efforts, the Gulf War broke out and Israel found itself under attack by long-range missiles.

The Americans had arrived in the Middle East to carry out a military offensive they labeled Desert Storm. It had commenced after Iraq, which had invaded the nation of Kuwait, ignored an American ultimatum demanding its withdrawal. On January 17, 1991, coalition forces moved in. This was a U.S.-Iraq conflict. Why then, was Israel under attack?

In the days prior to the war, Iraqi president Saddam Hussein had warned that any aggression toward Iraq would lead to an

Iraqi attack on Israel. Once again Israel prepared for war, but this time the preparation was uniquely different. Because it was feared that Iraq possessed chemical weapons and intended to use them, the Israeli people didn't need a standing army so much as they needed gasmasks. Distribution centers opened and families collected their gas masks and received instructions on how to protect themselves in case of an attack.

The first Iraqi Scud missiles landed in Tel Aviv and Haifa the day after Desert Storm began. For the next forty days of the Gulf War, thirty-nine missiles landed in Israel and others fell into the sea. Thousands of buildings were damaged, but the number of casualties was surprisingly low. The most dramatic result of the Iraqi attack was that this time Israel chose not to retaliate.

The decision, made by Israel in response to a specific American request, led some Arab countries to conclude that a military option to destroy Israel still existed. They interpreted Israeli restraint as weakness and lack of determination.

The Gulf War ignited a spark worldwide: many nations now recognized the need for a long-term solution in the Middle East. On October 30, 1991, a peace conference convened in Madrid, Spain. For the first time since Israel's independence, Israelis, Syrians, Jordanians, and Palestinians were seated around the same table, joined by the United States, Russia, the United Nations, and the European Union.

The issue at hand was the Israeli-Arab conflict. The Palestinian delegation had joined with the Jordanians as one group, since Israel refused to deal directly with the Palestinians. The conference did not bear immediate fruit; however, it appeared to be the impetus that both sides needed. The importance of the conference was better understood in later years when open negotiations were again held between Israel and her Arab neighbors.

In the 1992 elections, the Labor Party, behind Yitzhak Rabin, was chosen to lead the nation. Under Rabin's leadership (although at first against his will) Israel decided to initiate a peace process with the Palestinians: although the Israeli government had always refused to bow to terrorism, the Israeli public (after enduring years of random violence) was ready to pursue another tack and bring the conflict to an end.

Nonofficial talks were held between Israeli and Palestinian representatives in the Norwegian capital of Oslo. Israel had always refused to recognize the PLO as the legitimate representative of the Palestinian people; it now was willing to state otherwise. The PLO had previously refused to recognize the right of Israel to exist as a nation. That perspective had to be withdrawn. Only after these basic conditions were met did Rabin and Arafat exchange letters of mutual recognition. On September 13, 1993, at the White House in Washington D.C., the Declaration of Principles (the official title of the agreement forged in Oslo) was signed, heralding the hope of a new era in the Middle East.

The Oslo Accords were a courageous attempt made by former enemies to leave behind a legacy of hatred and bloodshed and work together for a better future. The gap between fundamental issues was unbridgeable, but the perspective of each party was as follows: agree on what was agreeable, leaving the tough issues (refugees, borders, Jerusalem) to the future. It was thought that the experience of living at peace with one another would reveal the benefits of peace to each, and lead to more flexibility on all sides.

The basic points covered in the agreement were:
- Autonomy for the Palestinians. (No specifics).
- Palestinian consent given to confront terrorists.
- Cessation of instigation by the Palestinian media.

- End of violence.
- A final agreement in five years (1998).

The common concept in the West was that the Israeli-Palestinian conflict stood at the core of the entire Israeli- Arab conflict, and added to the tension between the Arab world and the West. It was believed that this movement forward would create an atmosphere of calm in the Middle East and resolve many of the world's problems. (Writing today, more than ten years later, one can only be amazed at the naivety of all parties.)

Reaction from the public was mixed. Ever since 1967, the debate revolving around the territories was the axis upon which the Israeli political system turned. It was the "Great Divide" that polarized the Israeli public. The military evacuation of Israelis from the Sinai in 1982 and the sad spectacle of their demolished homes were acute memories still – many felt that the Oslo agreement would exact a similar painful price.

In an unusual move, the Declaration of Principles had been signed before it was submitted for a vote; the agreement still needed to come before the Knesset for approval. Since there was no significant majority for the plan in Parliament, those undecided, the "swing votes," were the targets of enormous pressure from both sides.

When the Knesset finally approved the Principles, a new era was supposed to begin in the Middle East. Israel implemented the agreement quickly, according to this understanding between the two sides: Gaza and Jericho first. On May 4, 1994, the Israeli forces pulled out of Jericho and on the 16th from Gaza City: taking the first step in what was to be the road to peace.

On July 1, 1994, Yasser Arafat, as chairman of the PLO and president of the Palestinian National Authority (PA), arrived in Gaza to set Palestinian autonomy into motion. (The PA had been established during the Oslo Accords as an interim governing body for the West Bank and the Gaza Strip. It was meant to oversee a limited form of Palestinian self-government for five years, until the final agreement expected in 1998 was realized. Arafat served as the PA's president from its inception in 1994 until his death in 2004.)

Problems surfaced immediately. The expectations on both sides were too high. The Israeli public had anticipated that Palestinian motivation for terrorism would decrease. The Palestinian people had hoped to establish an independent state and to see an immediate improvement in their financial condition. Both sides were soon disillusioned.

The Oslo Accords had altered the international climate regarding Israel. Since it seemed that peace was around the corner, many international businesses had moved in to take advantage of the improved conditions. Based on the new Middle Eastern atmosphere, matters also improved between Israel and neighboring countries; a peace treaty with Jordan was signed on October 26, 1994, and economic and other cooperation began to take place with other nations.

In contrast, the money that donor countries had been giving toward Palestinian autonomy began to be funneled to the PLO as the official representative of the PA. That money, intended for the construction of schools, roads and social improvements was used instead to pay wages to a corrupt regime that used most of it to strengthen its own position: twice as many policemen were recruited than the agreement permitted – mostly unskilled men who were relatives of the leadership. Discontent in Palestinian society continued to escalate – citizens were not ignorant as to how the donor money was being used. While the average Palestinian in the refugee camps lived a meager existence, in the Palestinian towns the officials had beautiful new buildings and many comforts.

Terrorism in Israel continued; bombs exploded on buses and in public places, killing dozens of people. Israel still believed that the PA was attempting to confront the terrorist groups on the Palestinian side. The PA's inability to stop the terrorism was attributed to a lack of organization. The reality sank slowly into the Israeli mindset: the Palestinians did not intend to honor their promises in the Oslo Accords.

Public opinion vacillated in Israel as the government wrestled with whether to honor its land-for-peace pledges, even as the PLO resolutely ignored its own promises inked on the Accords. The leaders of the two opposing camps gave passionate, incendiary speeches. Many Israelis felt that to cede land would be traitorous – and traitors should be punished. Religious leaders, normally reticent in matters of national policy, made an exception on this issue: many called on their disciples to rebel, even violently, against any decision in favor of releasing more land. Israel was on the verge of civil war, with the situation gradually sliding out of control.

Many citizens blamed Prime Minister Yitzhak Rabin for the increased terrorism and the growing number of Israeli victims. He became the main focus of anti-government demonstrations. On November 4, 1995, Rabin spoke at a rally in Tel Aviv supporting the peace agreement. Soon after finishing his speech, Rabin was gunned down on the way to his car.

Rabin's assassination stunned all of Israel. In their worst nightmares, the Israelis had not imagined such an event could be possible in their homeland. Voices daring to justify the murder, claiming that no man could make concessions for the entire nation, were roundly condemned by the majority.

This tragic event led to a comprehensive self-examination among national religious circles, which included most of the

Israelis who resided in the territories (where Rabin's assassin, an Orthodox Jew, had lived). Rabbis were called on to instruct religious Jews to draw the line at murder – and not cross it for any reason.

While things never got bad enough for a civil war, the Israeli public was frustrated to the extent that once again, the conservative Likud party, now led by Benjamin Netanyahu, was elected to lead the nation through the tough times ahead.

Along the northern border shared with Lebanon, an exchange of fire was ongoing. The Israeli Army was fighting shoulder-to-shoulder with the Christian South Lebanese army against the Hezbollah (the fanatic Iranian Muslim paramilitary organization based in Lebanon) and other Lebanese militias in "the Security Zone." The frequent skirmishes were a constant irritant. Israel suffered casualties but no Israeli civilians were injured or killed while the Israeli army was deployed in Lebanon.

South Lebanon was a restricted area, completely controlled by the Hezbollah. The Hezbollah was equipped with thousands of rockets of all kinds, threatening one-third of Israel's territory and population. Rockets were stored in houses, bunkers, and schools – populated areas. The Lebanese army and its police force stayed out of the Hezbollah's territory, following instructions from Tehran as well as from Damascus. Many questioned the Israeli government's decision to remain a presence in South Lebanon.

At home, another conflict took center stage: not so lethal, perhaps, but no less volatile. Jerusalem, the capital of the state and home to some seven hundred thousand people, is the largest city in Israel. About thirty five percent of the city's population can be categorized as Haredi (harh-ed'-ee) – ultra-Orthodox – Jews.

Such Jews have retained the centuries-old traditions of the Jewish faith, including dietary laws, strict observance of Jewish holy days, and a dress code that echoes the fashions of their ancestors. The Haredi consider that such things define their faith. They are an anachronism to the contemporary Jew, for ultra-Orthodox Judaism bears almost no resemblance to its modern counterpart.

The Haredi Jewish world within and without Israel has always had an uneasy relationship with the re-established state. As a secular democracy, Israel is far from meeting the expectations of the religious Orthodox world, which believes that the State must become completely rededicated to God and to the Mosaic Law.

The Haredi see their Orthodox lifestyle as threatened by the increasingly secular nature of modern Israel, and most Haredi Jews live in isolated quarters of Jerusalem and try to interact as little as possible with the rest of Israeli society.

For a long time, the Haredi refused to take part in political life, having been advised by their rabbis to avoid contact with the "Zionist entity." But when the Haredi Jews became unhappy with modern Israel's infringement upon their orthodox observances, they moved into the political arena by staging a protest. In this case, the unhappiness was due to traffic moving through Haredi neighborhoods on Jewish holidays and on the Sabbath – days on which the Orthodox Jew believes such activity is forbidden.

The roads in question were main thoroughfares. Closing them would affect many non-religious Jews, confining them in their neighborhoods or forcing them to take long detours to get to other parts of town. Most liberal Jews looked at changing the status quo (acceding to Haredi desires) as the first step down a very slippery slope.

For more than a month, every Sabbath day thousands of people stood lining the main roads: one side a dark ribbon of Haredi Jews, the men in traditional hats, beards, and long dark coats, the other side a colorful patchwork of modern Jews.

Hundreds of police officers stood along the routes, trying to maintain order as cars drove by.

Both sides were determined not to give up their position on the matter. As usual, a committee was appointed by the city, and instructed to come up with a workable compromise, which it did. To this day, during the Orthodox time of prayer and at certain other hours, the roads are blocked.

The Close of the Twentieth Century

The recently elected Likud government and its leader Netanyahu were in a tough position; the platform they had presented to the public before the recent elections was hard-line, opposed to any governmental concessions to achieve peace. Nevertheless, the State of Israel had already committed to the peace process and the new government could not withdraw from those commitments.

In January of 1997, Israeli forces evacuated Israelis from the Arab sections of the Palestinian city of Hebron (in Judea), retaining control only of the Jewish quarter. That was the last unilateral step taken by Israel; Netanyahu expected reciprocity from the Arabs and took the stance that without it, Israel had no further obligation toward the peace process. The message was at last understood on the Palestinian side, and for the first time Arafat moved to deliver some of the promises he had made through the Oslo Accords.

In 1998, Israel celebrated its fiftieth anniversary. Looking back to 1948, the people had every reason to be proud of what had been accomplished. Things were far from perfect, but Israel had been reborn against all odds – and survived and prospered against all expectations – in the nearly impossible conditions of the Middle East. That was certainly cause for celebration. Despite war, internal unrest, and terrorism, the population had grown to five and a half million. Israel's agricultural methods were some of the most advanced and productive in the world. While the challenges would continue to come, Israel's resilience in the past spoke well for its endurance in the future.

Israel Enters the 21st Century

On May 24, 2000, under the new Prime Minister Ehud Barak, Israel pulled completely out of Lebanon, fulfilling Barak's campaign promise that it would happen within a year of his election. The last Israeli soldier crossed the border back into Israel, closing the gate behind him.

Pulling out of Lebanon had complied with a requirement of the U.N.'s Security Council Resolution 425, and Israel expected that the other parties mentioned in the resolution would also comply: i.e., that after Israel's withdrawal, the Lebanese army would remove its forces from along their shared border.

Instead, the Hezbollah began occupying former Israeli positions along the border, presenting a new threat instead of removing the old one. In order to guarantee that Israel's withdrawal would end any territorial conflict, and to ensure that Israel was in fact not occupying any Lebanese territory, Israel asked the U.N. to mark the new border between the two countries.

Once the northern border was less of a hotspot, Israel could turn its attention to the Palestinian issue. An offer was formulated based on what Israel thought were Palestinian expectations. In July of 2000, at Camp David, Maryland, the Israeli Prime Minister met with Yasser Arafat, still the Chairman of the Palestinian National Authority. Israel proposed total withdrawal from ninety-three percent of the territories. A

Palestinian state would be established with East Jerusalem as its capital. To compensate for the seven percent Israel would keep, especially around Jerusalem, land from Israel proper (around the Gaza Strip) would be transferred to the Palestinians. The only issue on which Israel was not willing to compromise was the right of return for Palestinian refugees. It was a great disappointment when Arafat refused the offer.

Some still question even today why the Israeli offer was rejected. It is possible that Israel's withdrawal from Lebanon two months previously was interpreted in the Arab world as a Hezbollah victory. If so, the Arabs perhaps felt no need to make any agreements with or concessions to Israel, believing that they could soon claim militarily whatever they desired nationally.

With no resolution in sight for the Israeli-Palestinian question, tension mounted. The failure of the peace talks turned public opinion away from Barak and also discredited the validity of the entire peace process.

On September 28, 2000, the leader of the Likud party, Ariel Sharon, visited Temple Mount in Jerusalem (still under the jurisdiction of the Arabs). Such a visit might not normally have drawn much attention, but the times were not normal. Many Arabs saw the visit as a clear provocation. In a very short time the violence spread, and the conflict came to be known as the Al-Aqsa Intifadah.

Since the Palestinians refused to disarm or dismantle the Hamas, and continued to promote Islamic Jihad, Israel retaliated: After warnings that were ignored, the Arab infrastructure was bombed (headquarters, police stations etc.). Palestinians who were employed in Israel continued to show up for work in large numbers, nearly a hundred thousand every day. Only after some of these workers brought in bombs that exploded in public places was this privilege significantly restricted.

Both the United States and the European Union made an effort to promote a ceasefire and resume peace talks. U.S. senator Dennis Mitchell was sent, followed by C.I.A. director George Tannet, to bring both parties to the table. It looked as if the talks would actually accomplish something, but the conflict grew rapidly out of control. The PA was unable or unwilling to corral the Palestinian gangs and militias, which competed with each other in a race to kill the most Israelis.

With no effective Palestinian effort to contain terrorism, Israel began searching out Palestinian terrorists, eradicating them in what is called "Target Killing." Still, Israel did not invade Palestinian territory

By 2002 the number of Israelis killed in terror attacks had climbed to one hundred and sixty three. Israel decided to "take the gloves off," and on March 28, Operation Defensive Shield was launched. The invasion took the Palestinian terrorists by surprise; they had believed that Israel would hesitate to enter the serpentine maze of the Casbahs (market places) to search them out. Expecting an attack on the refugee camps instead, the terrorists had booby-trapped the camps and positioned local citizens as human shields.

Israeli forces did not spring the trap: they avoided the camps and invaded the Palestinian cities, hunting down terrorist masterminds and seizing documents proving that Palestinian officials were party to the terrorism. Arafat's compound in Ram Allah was blockaded, primarily for symbolic reasons, as it was the center of Palestinian sovereignty.

It now seemed pointless to Israel to engage in further talks or seek additional agreements, as the Palestinians had proven uninterested in following through with anything that had been expected from them. After Operation Defensive Shield, Israel penetrated Palestinian holdings whenever it believed there was a need to do so; it had indeed "taken the gloves off."

Side by side with these military encroachments, Prime Minister Ariel Sharon presented a new strategy – physical separation. The plan spoke of a unilateral disengagement while building a security fence to separate Israeli and Palestinian territories – although two hundred thousand Israelis would then reside behind the fence.

The logic behind the plan was to show the world that Israel meant business and would not wait around for the Arabs to belatedly fulfill their promises. With Israel initiating this first step, the pressure would be on the Palestinians to prove to the world whether they were truly willing to work for peace.

In making the decision to create a physical barrier, several issues were examined. Many were concerned about the Israelis living in Palestinian territory. However, more than 1.3 million Palestinians surrounded the Israeli communities in the Gaza area. From a practical standpoint, it had never been possible for Israel to guarantee the protection of Jews residing in the territories. The erection of a physical barrier would not endanger a safety that had never even been achieved. The effect on the army was also considered: forming a clear line of defense, rather than relying on scattered outposts, would significantly reduce the manpower needed for border defense and allow efficient patrol of the Israeli side.

During 2003-2004, the work on the fence continued. Success was immediate – wherever it existed, terrorism was reduced to nearly zero. The critics began to fall silent and support for the project increased. The Palestinians refused to recognize it, since it was a unilateral Israeli decision, but Israel was about to pull out from the Gaza Strip, and that was certainly what the Palestinians wanted.

In Israel however, the plan caused trouble for Sharon: it contradicted his stated platform as presented during the election campaign, and many who had voted for him were unhappy. Sharon and his family were also suspected of financial irregularity and the opposition had accused him of initiating the disengagement in a maneuver designed to save his own skin.

On November 11, 2004, Yasser Arafat died in a hospital outside Paris, France. His successor, Mahmud Abas (Abu Mazin) called for the cessation of terrorism against Israel on several occasions, an approach that was more than welcome to Israel. When Abas was elected as Chairman of the PA, it seemed possible that the peace process could begin anew. However, even if the new leader was sincere, too much power was now in the hands of the Hamas, a group unwilling to concede anything for peace. In fact, as Israel prepared to withdraw from the Gaza Strip, the Hamas claimed that the withdrawal was due to Israel's terror of that fierce organization.

On August 15, 2005, the orchestrated withdrawal began. In the space of a few days, some eight thousand Jewish settlers were evacuated from their homes in the Gaza Strip and four communities in northern Samaria. The evacuation reminded every Israeli of the forced withdrawal from the Sinai in 1982. Houses and synagogues (after the scrolls of the Torah were removed) were leveled to the ground. Greenhouses containing the most sophisticated equipment in the world were destroyed. The life's work of over a thousand families, in the area for thirty-five years, came to an end. It was a heartbreaking process in which Israeli civilians and soldiers stood on opposite sides.

If there was hope in Israel that the action would completely stop terrorism, it was a vain hope. The fence is extremely effective and terrorists now find it very hard to penetrate into Israel. However, the fence cannot stop rockets. Ever since Israel has pulled out of Gaza, thousands of rockets have fallen on Israeli communities near the Gaza Strip. Not surprisingly, after the disengagement the Hamas (being given and taking credit for Israel's withdrawal) was elected to power in the PA in January of 2006. The Hamas has never recognized any of the agreements the PA had signed with Israel, and does not recognize Israel's right to exist.

Israel is one of very few nations that possess the technology to build satellites for intelligence and other purposes. This gives the country an obvious advantage in regional conflicts. According to foreign sources, Israel also has nuclear weapons, but Israel has never officially admitted this, defining its nuclear policy by the statement: "Israel will not be the first country in the Middle East to use nuclear weapons."

A real threat is emerging in the east. Iran for years has been applying its resources toward obtaining nuclear capacity. The Ayatollahs speak openly about Iran's nuclear research, Iran's right to possess such weapons, and how Iran intends to use them. Israel should be concerned.

Today, Israel finds itself with a good international reputation, the recipient of worldwide approval for the disengagement and for future plans in the same spirit. Since the election of the Hamas to power in the PA, the world is boycotting the PA and demanding that they take action to halt the arsenal of rockets being launched into Israel. The country has not enjoyed such support since the years preceding the Six Day War. Then the sympathy was given because of Israel's weakness and isolation – it is given now in recognition of Israel's strength.

In recent elections in Israel, the new Kadima party presented a concept it had been established specifically to promote: a large-scale disengagement in Judea and Samaria. As with the first action, Israel will enter into no negotiations, since the Palestinian leadership refuses to recognize Israel's existence or to halt terrorism.

Based on this plan, the Kadima Party won the elections. Ehud Olmert, who had become acting Prime Minister after Sharon suffered a stroke, now officially represented his party as Prime Minister of Israel. While the preliminary steps for implementing the new disengagement plans took place, a war broke out on Israel's northern border that changed the course of events.

The Hezbollah, with massive Iranian and Syrian assistance, had been training and equipping an efficient guerilla force on Israel's northern border. On July 12, 2006, Hezbollah terrorists crossed Israel's border and ambushed an Israeli patrol. During the attack, in which two soldiers were abducted and three were killed, hundreds of rockets were fired at Israeli towns along the border to divert attention from what was really going on.

The assault triggered an Israeli attack on the Hezbollah in Lebanon. It was an unusual war in several ways – it was not a war between two countries, and Israel did whatever was possible to avoid attacking Lebanese targets. The enemy was operating from houses, schools, and hospitals, using the locals as human shields.

Hundreds of rockets were shot at Israel daily for over a month. One million Israelis were forced to live in bomb shelters, many of which were not equipped for the need. Hundreds of thousands of Israelis left the northern region, forced to seek refuge elsewhere.

Israel was not prepared for this type of war. Years of dealing with terrorism required a specific readiness that did not translate well to a broader threat. The hope that the Israeli Air Force could solve the problem was proven wrong; a ground operation was necessary to destroy the Hezbollah's infrastructure. Such an operation required calling in the reserves. With much hesitation, and only a day after the ground operation had begun, a ceasefire brought the “mini war” to an end.

The Hezbollah lost most of its military power, its bases, and its infrastructure in south Lebanon. Most importantly, it lost the support of many Lebanese. The “Protector of Lebanon” as the Hezbollah liked to be called, had brought massive destruction on Lebanon with nothing good to show for it.

As these words are written, only a few weeks after the war’s end, there are some positive signs from Israel's perspective. The Hezbollah is no longer along Israel's border, and the Lebanese army, along with a multi-national task force, is deployed in south Lebanon.

In Israel, although it had used only a small part of its military capability, many problems were identified: the rear was no longer sufficiently protected and its resilience was put to the test. A lot of work is necessary in order to be better prepared for the next round.

Many experts believe that this was the first battle in what might develop into a global war when and if Iran possesses nuclear capabilities. Israel continues to make its way forward from war to war and from one terrorist attack to another. One can only imagine how much more could be accomplished in Israel if the money dedicated to maintaining a standing army and other security needs were instead available for such things as education, agriculture, and medical research.

Because of the seemingly endless efforts needed to repel those who covet the land and hate its people, one might gain the impression that Israel’s modern history is only a litany of wars, bloodshed, and death. There is no bigger mistake than to portray life in Israel in such a manner. Despite the ongoing challenges, today’s Israel is a progressive country with a vital society and a strong economy. Tourism flourishes. Universities and colleges are full of students, and Israel's medical community enjoys worldwide acclaim. The very desert has been conquered and made green.

While these achievements of the present are indeed important, Modern Israel has also honored the responsibility to preserve its past: museums are filled with the proof of a rich and deep history.

Now Israel looks to the future.

19

The Future of Israel

Both Christians and Jews note the year 1948, the year that Israel was declared a nation, as the fulfillment of a promise God had made to Israel thousands of years before:

> *"Therefore say: 'This is what the Sovereign LORD says: Although I sent them far away among the nations and scattered them among the countries, yet for a little while I have been a sanctuary for them in the countries where they have gone.' "Therefore say: 'This is what the Sovereign LORD says: I will gather you from the nations and bring you back from the countries where you have been scattered, and I will give you back the land of Israel again.' "(Ezekiel 11:16-17)*

No matter your perspective, the re-establishment of Israel as an independent nation is something that heralds great things in the eyes of both Jew and Christian. Both believe that the coming of the Messiah (for the Jew, the first arrival, for the Christian, the second arrival of Jesus Christ) could not take place until the nation was back in the land.

More than seven million people call Israel home. Despite the many differences in Israeli society, there is one thing that almost all will agree upon: the re-gathering of the Jews in Israel is indeed the fulfillment of Biblical prophecy – the God of Israel had gathered his people from among the nations and brought them home.

> *This is what Isaiah son of Amos saw concerning Judah and Jerusalem: In the last days the mountain of the LORD's temple will be established as chief among the mountains; it will be raised above the hills, and all nations will stream to it. Many peoples will come and say, 'Come, let us go up to the mountain of the LORD, to the house of the God of Jacob. He will teach us his ways, so that we may walk in his paths.' The law will go out from Zion, the word of the LORD from Jerusalem. He will judge between the nations and will settle disputes for many peoples. They will beat their swords into ploughshares and their spears into pruning hooks. Nation will not take up sword against nation, nor will they train for war any more. Come, O house of Jacob, let us walk in the light of the LORD. (Isaiah 2:1-5)*

And He is not done with us yet.

Chronology of events

Chronology for chapter two – The Canaanite Era

The 18th-19th B.C.	–	the era of the Patriarchs.
Circa 1440 B.C.	–	the Exodus.
Circa 1300 B.C.	–	Pharaoh Setti the 3rd campaign in Can'an.
Circa 1290	–	Battle of Qedesh between the Egyptians and the Hittites.
Circa 1207 B.C.	–	Pharaoh Merneptah's campaign in Can'an.
1050 B.C.	–	The battle of Eben-Ezer, the Philistines conquer Israel.
1250-1020 B.C.	–	The era of the judges.

Chronology for chapter three – The Monarchy

1020 B.C.	–	Saul is anointed king by the prophet Samuel.
1000 B.C.	–	Saul is killed in battle against the Philistines on Mount Gilboa.
1000 B.C.	–	David is made king over Judah and six years later Over all of Israel.
960 B.C.	–	The death of David, replaced by Solomon.
953 B.C.	–	The dedication of Solomon's Temple in Jerusalem.

920 B.C.	– The death of Solomon. Kingdom divides; Judah in the south and Israel in the north. An Egyptian invasion under Pharaoh Shishak.
722 B.C.	– Sargon 2nd, king of Assyria conquers Samaria. End of northern kingdom of Israel and exile.
701 B.C.	– The Assyrian army besieges Jerusalem and fails to capture the city.
605 B.C.	– The battle of Carchemish. The Babylonian army defeats the Egyptians.

Chronology for chapter four – Removed and Returned

586 B.C.	– Nebuchadnezzar 2nd, king of Babylon captures Jerusalem, destroys the Temple and exiles the people.

The aftermath of the exile – the return to Jerusalem.
The Babylonian & Persian eras. 586 B.C.– 332 B.C.

539 B.C.	– Cyrus' declaration allows Jewish exiles to return to Judah and rebuild the temple.
520 B.C.	– Building the second temple in Jerusalem begins.
515 B.C.	– Dedication of the second Temple.

Chronology for chapter five – Various Overlords

332 B.C.	– Alexander's army conquers Judea.
323 B.C.	– The death of Alexander the great. Israel in the hand of Thalami king of Egypt.
223 B.C.	– Antiochus 3rd begins his reign in Syria and Thalami 4th, in Syria.
218 B.C.	– Antiochus invades Israel. Stopped by Thalami in Rapha.

200 B.C. – The battle at Banyas; A Syrian victory. Israel under the Seleucid dynasty.

Chronology for chapter six – The Rise and Fall of the Hasmoneans

167 B.C. – The beginning of the Jewish revolt led by Matthathias the Hasmonean.

161 B.C. – Roman recognition in the Jewish kingdom. The death of Judah Maccabeus.

152 B.C.-143 B.C. – Jonathan, Judah's brother leads the revolt.

143 B.C.-135 B.C. – Simeon, establishes an independent Kingdom and is titled "the head of the Jews."

135 B.C.-104 B.C. – John (Yohanan) Hyrcanus expends the kingdom's territory to Edumea, Samaria and the coast.

104 B.C.-103 B.C.– Judah Aristoblus conquers Galilee.

103 B.C-76 B.C. – Alexander Yaneus' reign.

76 B.C.-67 B.C. – Shlomzion's, Alexander's wife reign.

67 B.C.-63 B.C. – Civil war in Judea.

63 B.C. – Pompeii "the great" conquers Jerusalem. Beginning of Roman era.

Chronology for chapter 7 – The Edumean rulers

47 B.C. – Herod Appointed Governor of Galilee.

40 B.C. – Antigonus, with Persian support, conquers Jerusalem and proclaimed King.

37 B.C. – Herod resumes power with Rome's help.

30 B.C. – The battle of Actium – The death of Mark Anthony.

4 B.C. – The death of Herod. The kingdom is divided among his three sons.

6 A.D.	– Archelaos, Herod's son and governor of Judea and Samaria sent to exile. Judea proclaimed province.

Chronology for chapter 8 – The "Great Revolt"

37 – 44 A.D.	– The reign of Agrippa I.
37-41 A.D.	– The reign of Caligula.
41 -54 A.D.	– The reign of Claudius.
66 A.D.	– Beginning of the Jewish revolt.
68 A.D.	– The death of Nero. The year of the four Caesars.
70 A.D.	– The conquest of Jerusalem. Destruction of the Temple and exile.

Chronology for chapter 9 – After the Great Revolt

117-138	– Hadrian's reign.
132-135	– The Bar Kochva revolt.
138-161	– Antoninus Pius' reign.
Circa 200	– The completion of the Mishnah – the Jewish Oral Law.

Chronology for chapter 10 – The Byzantine Era

October, 312	– Constantine's, the Emperor of the west.
September, 324	– Constantine reunites the Roman Empire.
325	– The Council of Nicaea.
May, 330	– The dedication of Constantinople.
351	– The Galus revolt.
361-363	– The reign of Julian "The Apostate".
411	– The Empress Eudokiah moves to Jerusalem.
429	– Abolishing the office of Perfectos.
451	– The council of Chalcedon.

484, 529	– Samaritan revolts.
527 – 565	– The reign of Justinian.
603	– Persia invades Byzantium.
May, 614	– Jerusalem is conquered by Persia.
March, 629	– Byzantine Emperor Heraclius conquers Jerusalem.

Chronology for chapter 11 – The Early Muslim Era

634-638	– The Byzantine – Muslim war over Israel.
661	– Muawiyyah, founding the Umayyad dynasty.
692	– The "Dome of the Rock" is constructed.
705	– The mosque of "Al – Aqsa" is constructed.
750	– Abas' rebellion.
970	– Israel under Fatimide occupation.
1009	– The church of the Holy Sepulcher is destroyed by the Fatimides.
1030	– The restoration of the church by Byzantium.

Chronology for chapter 12 – Introduction to the Crusades

1054	– the Great Schism.
November, 1095	– Pope Urban's appeal.
1096 – 1099	– The armies of the first crusade journey to Palestine.
July, 1099	– The conquest of Jerusalem. Founding the "Latin Kingdom of Jerusalem".

Chronology for chapter 13 – The First Latin Kingdom

December, 1144	– The conquest of Edessa. The first Latin kingdom that was lost to the Muslims.

1148 – The second crusade leaves little mark in Palestine.

1153 – The conquest of Ashkelon.

1183 – Sladin unites Egypt and Syria under his dominance.

July, 1187 – The battle at the Horns of Hittin. The crusaders loose the Kingdom.

October, 1187 – Jerusalem taken by Saladin.

Chronology for chapter 14 – The second Latin Kingdom

1191 – The armies of the third crusade reach Palestine.

September, 1192 – Establishing the Second Latin Kingdom.

1229 – Fredrick gains control over Jerusalem.

1239 – The "Barons crusade".

1240 – Richard of Cornwell arrives in Palestine.

May, 1249 – The army of King Louis 9th lands on the shores of Egypt.

Chronology for chapter 15 – The Mamelukes

September, 1260 – the battle of Ein-Jalut. The Mongol defeat.

1260 – Bybars, the Mameluk is made Sultan.

1265 – The fall of Caesarea.

1268 – The fall of Antioch.

1272 – Crown prince Edward of England leads the nine's crusade.

1289 – The fall of the Earldom of Tripoli, Lebanon.

May, 1291 – Acre, the capital of the kingdom conquered.

August, 1291 – The last crusader fortress abounded. The end of the Latin Kingdom.

1517 – The Ottomans conquer Israel.

Chronology for chapter 16 – The Ottoman Era

1520-1566	– The reign of Suleiman "The Magnificent".
1535	– Trade benepits are granted to France in Ottoman territory as well as representing Catholic interests.
1635	– Fahar A-Din executed.
1774	– Russia is recognized as the protector of Christian Orthodox interests in the Ottoman Empire.
1775	– Death of Dahr El-Omar.
1798	– Napoleon's army lands in Egypt.
March-May, 1799	– The French army besiege Acre.
1804	– The death of Ahmed Jazzar.
1832	– Israel taken by Muhammad Ali, the Pasha of Egypt.
1840	– The Egyptian army evacuates Israel.
1854-1856	– The "Crimean War".
1869	– The opening of the Suez Canal.
1882	– Great Britain conquers Egypt.
1897	– The birth of the Zionist movement.
1898	– The visit of the German Emperor, William II.
1914-1918	– WWI
1917	– The "Balfour declaration".
September, 1918	– The Ottoman troops evacuate Israel.

Chronology for chapter 17 – The British Mandate

1920	– The official beginning of the British Mandate.
1922	– The "white Paper" – Trans-Jordan given to prince Abdullah.
1936-1939	– The Arab Revolt.
1937	– The "Royal Commission" publishes its report.
May, 1939	– Mc Donald's "White Paper".
1939-1945	– WWII.

February, 1947 – Britain returns the mandate to the United Nations.
November 29, 1947 – The U.N's General Assembly votes for resolution 181.

Chronology for chapter 18 – The State of Israel

November, 1947 – May, 1948, The Israeli-Palestinian war.
May 14, 1948 – Termination of the British Mandate. The birth of the State of Israel.
July 1949 – The end of The War of Independence.
October 1956 – The "Suez war".
May, 1962 – Adolph Eichman execution.
June 1967 – The "Six Day War".
1967-1970 – "The War of Attrition".
October, 1973 – The "Yom Kippur" war.
November, 1977 – Sadat's visit to Jerusalem.
March, 26, 1979 – The Israeli-Egyptian peace accord signed.
1982 – Israel pulls out of the Sinai.
June, 1982 – Israel invades Lebanon to uproot the PLO.
December 1987 – The "Intifadah", the Palestinian uprising.
January, 1991 – The Gulf War.
October, 1991 – The Madrid conference.
September, 1993 – The "Declaration of Principles" is signed in Washington D.C.
May, 1994 – Israel pulls out of Jericho and Gaza.
July, 1994 – The formation of the Palestinian Authority.
October, 1994 – Peace with Jordan.
November, 4, 1995 – The assassination of Yitzhak Rabin.
May, 2000 – Israel pulls out of Lebanon.
October, 2000 – Beginning of the Al Aqsa Intifadah.
August, 2005 – Israel pulls out of Gaza.
July-August, 2006 – The "Second Lebanese War."